T0266124

Owsley and Me

OWSLEY AND ME
My LSD Family

Rhoney Gissen Stanley
with
Tom Davis

Monkfish Book Publishing Company
Rhinebeck, New York

Owsley and Me: My LSD Family
© 2012 Rhoney Gissen Stanley and Tom Davis

All rights reserved. No part of this book may be used or
reproduced in any manner without written permission from
the publisher except in critical articles and reviews. Contact
the publisher for information.

Printed in the United States of America

Library of Congress Cataloging-in-Publication Data

Gissen-Stanley, Rhoney.
   Owsley and me : my LSD family / Rhoney Gissen-Stanley and Tom Davis.
      pages cm
   ISBN 978-0-9833589-3-0 (alk. paper)
   ISBN: 978-098335-894-7 (ebook)
   1. LSD (Drug)--Social aspects--United States--History. 2. Drug abuse--
United States--History. I. Davis, Tom. II. Title.
   HV5822.5.L9G57 2013
   362.29'4092--dc23
   [B]

                         2013000166

Book cover design by Lauren Manoy
   based on a photograph by Alvan Meyerowitz

Book interior design by Bill McAllister

The authors and publisher gratefully acknowledge and thank the following
artists for permission to use their work in *Owsley and Me*:

Featuring the photographs of Alvan Meyerowitz on pages x, 5, 128, 137,
138, 139, 140, 141, 144, 145, 146, 207, 269
Blue Bailey for his photograph on page 141
Corbis Images for use of their photograph on page 143
Alex Grey for use of his painting on page 96
Robert Hunter for use of his poem on pages 266-267
Jean Millay for use of her photograph on page 138
Rosie McGee for use of her photographs on pages 6, 32, 139, 142
Amalie R. Rothschild for use her photograph on page 142
Tim Scully for use of his drawing on page 51
Stanley Mouse for use of his artwork on page 156

Monkfish Book Publishing Company
22 E. Market St., Suite 304 Rhinebeck, NY 12572
www.monkfishpublishing.com

Thank you to the people I have known and loved
who made my life so interesting
that I felt compelled to write about it.

Thanks for sharing the music
and the spirit of community.

Thank you for helping me create more joy.

Table of Contents

Foreword

In this first outdoor party of 2008, it turned into one of those slow New England soakers, and hail herded us all into the large-beamed, screened-in, fireplace-lit porch. In the far corner I saw this woman who saw me seeing her, and her eyes told me SHE HAD DONE THE ACID. I was intrigued. Smiling, I made my way through the wet, wooly crowd and sat where she made room for me on the couch.

"Hi—I'm Tom Davis."

"I know. You're Jon McIntire's friend." Indeed, our common friend had also been the Grateful Dead's road manager twice. As it turned out, Rhoney had not only DONE the acid, she'd MADE the acid under the tutelage of Owsley Stanley. She had been a lab technician for the skeleton crew who produced an estimated two million hits to fuel the Northern California psychedelic revolution of the sixties. Her experience with the Grateful Dead was ending just as mine was beginning in 1971.

Ironically, I don't believe I ever met Owsley Stanley, the man of Rhoney's life.

This chronicle of Rhoney's life stories benefited from my own recent experience writing my memoir, plus I've been a writer in show business for forty years. As a first-time coauthor, she walked into this door without knowing about the agony and the artistry that would drive us both nuts during the next three years.

Writing for women has always been a challenge for me—and Rhoney is a feminine force. Our collaboration has been the oddest kind of success, but I am as proud of this as anything I've ever done. She's been the goose laying the golden eggs while wondering, what are these strange, cold, gleaming yellow things.

Tom Davis

Rhoney Gissen, student days at UC Berkeley   © Alvan Meyerowitz

Neti Neti: Neither This Nor That

No music was playing on the car radio as we drove onto the Mount Holyoke College campus. I cringed in the backseat, small as I was, slumped down, wishing for invisibility, embarrassed to be arriving for my freshman year at college in a big car driven by a black man in a chauffeur's hat. My mother couldn't take time from her busy schedule of luncheons to drive me to college and had sent me with my grandmother's chauffeur. We checked in at the front desk of Mary Lyon Hall, a nineteenth-century stone building covered in ivy.

My roommate was six feet tall, from Kenilworth, Illinois, the Gold Coast suburb of Chicago with country clubs where Jews were restricted from membership. Different in many ways, we both couldn't tolerate the Tuesday and Thursday morning mandatory chapel, the signing in and signing out, the dress code for dinner, the eleven o'clock curfew, the bell that chimed every fifteen minutes, ringing so many hours of the day that it became a normal sound—a ringing that was part of being, an accustomed anxiety.

Smoking was only allowed in designated smoking rooms, and here I found my place. I took a dare to go drinking with the girls at a town pub. I furtively left the dorm in a short skirt and high-heeled boots and joined the other girls at the bus stop. The local bar smelled like stale cigarettes, alcohol, and urine; I chain-smoked Marlboros that I bummed off the upperclassmen, laughed loudly,

and raised my Black Russian in besotted camaraderie.
To sneak back into the dorm, I crept through an open
window and knocked over a glass vase on the windowsill.
It shattered on the floor and woke up the House Mother.
She shook her finger and threatened me with a hearing
before the student–faculty board.

Mount Holyoke was on the honor system, and I
told the truth. The following week the House Mother
called me into her office and handed me an envelope
addressed to me with the Mount Holyoke seal, a picture
of palm trees, mountains, and a small building, dated
1837. It quoted Psalm 144:12: "Our daughters may be
as cornerstones polished after the similitude of a palace."
I did not open the letter in front of her and left without
saying anything. In my dorm room, sitting on the narrow
bed, I read the verdict of the Board. They had judged me
harshly. I was put on disciplinary probation and required
to see the college psychiatrist.

In an office at the infirmary, the doctor sat behind a
desk wearing a white jacket, her hair in a perfect coiffure.
She spoke with a stern voice: I broke the rules; I did
not understand the value of tradition; I was too easily
influenced; I needed to obey authority. This shrink had
no respect for thinking outside the box. It was obvious
I would have to transfer. I considered the University
of Chicago where Robert Hutchins had instituted the
Great Books program whose mission was to teach the
responsibility of citizenship. But the University of
California at Berkeley was the hottest hotbed of political
action, and it was as far away from my family as I could
get, psychiatrically.

I didn't have far to look for "alternative lifestyles"
in Berkeley, California. Outside the administration

building on Sproul Plaza, students gathered at the Fountain to exchange ideas and discuss the escalating attack on Vietnam by the Kennedy administration. The more forthright ones set up tables at Bancroft Way and Telegraph Avenue on the edge of campus and distributed leaflets denouncing war and calling the administration fascist pigs. My new roommates were "Red diaper babies," the daughters of Red Communist American parents. We protested US policy on Vietnam and Cuba. We marched in black pumps with little heels and skirts with hemlines that ended below the knees and bras to keep our boobs from jiggling.

Thus began a streak of nightly meetings to plan a strategy to end the Vietnam War. If you felt the urge, you could stand in front of the group and speak your mind. I was shocked that several advocated violence. One decent guy with a Lenin T-shirt and ponytail stood up and yelled, "Bullshit! We don't need guns to make change!" We brought him home and his buddy tagged along. We put on a Ray Charles record and danced. Left-wing politics was very sexy.

In the morning we made omelets with brie and bean sprouts. Another roommate's boyfriend sat astride a reversed chair at the kitchen table. Dressed in fatigues, his blonde hair short in the military style, he sipped Jamaican Blue Mountain out of my favorite coffee cup and started his revolutionary spiel. His voice was deep and he spoke intently, as if he were confiding an important secret. "There is no peaceful solution to the struggle. The only way to defeat the capitalist pigs is to shoot them. It's just not wise to say so yet."

I thought, what the fuck is he doing sitting at my table? I wanted to change the complacency of societal beliefs but not with violence.

The more I went to meetings, the more disillusioned
I became. The Students for a Democratic Society, the
Socialist Workers Party, both were too rigid, too alpha, too
much a man's movement. I soon learned that these left-
wing politicos were all the same in bed. They wanted a
blowjob and that was it. If watching them come off didn't
give you an orgasm, you were frigid. Maybe that's where
their politics came from.

One night, fifteen women got together and held a
meeting—just the girls. We were good students at UC
Berkeley, aiming for Phi Beta Kappa. We did not look
like militant feminists. I wore a black miniskirt and tights,
dressed up as much for the chicks as if I were going to a
hot party. We clinked wine glasses and the meeting came
to order. We started our own exchange about stuff that
mattered to us.

"When I wiggle my diaphragm slips out," I confided to
one woman.

She laughed. "Mine slips out when I get wet—great
advancement for womankind! And birth control pills
make me fat. What do you think of the IUD? It's got the
best stats in terms of effectiveness."

"Overpopulation is the source of all the world's
problems," I singsonged to her.

"Then the IUD is a real solution," she spat out fiercely.

"The idea of a foreign object in my uterus is more than
unappealing to me," I replied.

A butch dyke with short boyish hair and a stocky build
expounded the virtues of lesbianism. "Men don't take
women seriously. I want them to think about right and
wrong, and I want them to fear."

My friend Susie Griffin did not blink her true blue
eyes and spoke with intensity. "Men act as if they possess

women. Possession creates the inequality of women and leads to men's mistreatment of women. The way women are treated determines the social hierarchy of a society. Men have no sense. They don't know about women's multiple erotic zones. They only focus on sexual intercourse."

"Men have their feminine side, too," I offered in an appeasing voice.

"But they don't respect it," she countered. "Other women know instinctively what a woman wants, but men never ask. They are too macho and self-involved."

I thought to myself, this is not the kind of chick I want to be.

Antiwar protest, San Francisco Civic Center, CA   © Alvan Meyerowitz

Owsley Stanley, May 1966

© Rosie McGee

The Lure of Chemistry

Charles and I sat at a small table downstairs at the Mediterranean Café on Telegraph Avenue. I sipped my cappuccino as he wept. Wallowing in despair, rubbing his bald head, he looked like the egg man. Love lost, tears ran down his face. The Berkeley women's movement had claimed another victim. His wife had dropped him for another woman.

Our conversation was interrupted by the roar of motorcycles from the street. Several bikers entered and a big guy with a bushy beard and an Oakland Hell's Angel jacket pointed at Charles, who wiped away his tears and smiled. The biker walked up and slapped him on the back. Charles's voice assumed a deeper bravado as he stood and hugged his biker friend.

I left them and mounted the stairs for the ladies' room on the second floor. I heard an acoustic guitar playing a familiar tune. A guy in an embroidered Mexican shirt was playing at one of the small round Italian marble tables. He was good. His intense beady eyes were lost in the song. His fingers deftly picked the nylon strings. He stopped and looked up at me. "People only come upstairs to use the bathroom or to get lost." He spoke with a slight German accent and nodded his head at me. "Hi! My name is Perry."

I smiled. "I'm not lost but give me a minute."

He laughed. "I'll be here." Indeed he was.

After a cappuccino, we went to his apartment around the corner. It was a nice space with a Turkish rug, a

mahogany coffee table, and lots of large paisley pillows.
With great pride, he showed me his record collection.
We listened to the Swan Silvertones, an a cappella gospel
group, and then we made love. I still have that record. I
think he gave it to me.

A few days later we took a trip to the Mendocino coast
in his lime green VW Bug. We turned off onto a small
road to the beach, and the car promptly got stuck in the
sand. After some futile spinning of the wheels, he shut off
the engine and we got out to watch the crashing waves.

"Let's take LSD," he said, as he took a prescription pill
bottle out of his leather shoulder purse. He handed me a
capsule and a bottle of water. I swallowed. So did he.

The car radio played "Hey, Mr. Tambourine Man."
Dylan's words flowed like the tide. I floated in my new
consciousness. The sun set over the Pacific Ocean, and
it was like seeing colors for the first time. I witnessed the
merging of water and sky, the infinity of the universe, the
changing of perspective. We made love under the stars. I
swayed with the to and fro of the ocean waves as the sun
rose behind us, and I could feel the roundness of the Earth.

The high I had reached on this LSD was different.

"Where did you get this acid?" I asked.

"It's Owsley acid, the best," Perry told me.

When the sun came up we headed back to the Bug, still
immersed in the sand. Perry started the engine and rocked
the car forward and backward until the tires gained
traction, and we made our way back to the road.

Later, I lay on Perry's bed while he played his guitar. As
his fingers fondled the strings, his playing struck a chord in
me. Maybe that's why musicians make good lovers, I thought.

My mother had told me if I slept around, no man
would want me as his wife. When I was ten years old,

I watched my mother as she dressed up in sexy black lingerie and stockings and pranced before the mirror. My father was due home from work at any minute. When we heard his car pull into the driveway, she put on her regular clothes, went downstairs, and verbally abused the old milquetoast. There was no sex. I didn't want to be a wife. Being a good lover was enough.

Perry wanted sex but he couldn't get it up, so he begged for a blowjob. I thought about it. He was smart, a good musician, but addicted to speed.

He said, "Owsley's bringing over a Sennheiser for me to try, a German microphone." There was dignity in his voice. He was a Jew but first call him a proud German, a proud German Jew, a proud German Jew speed freak with snobbery in his conceit.

"When will he get here?" I asked.

"He'll get here when he gets here—on Owsley time!"

He arrived several hours later. When Perry opened the door, a man breezed into the apartment like a hippie Dracula. He was small but muscular with long brown hair and a straight patrician nose. Immediately, I felt chemistry between us. He focused on me.

"Call me Bear." He flexed his muscles in an exaggerated posture of a comic book character. "I'm a Bear." I laughed. He smiled and took a small, unmarked brown bottle out of his vest pocket, turned to Perry, and looked him in the eye.

"Do not expose my name to the world. Do not say 'Owsley acid.' If you do not pay attention, this will be the last LSD you will see from me."

The tips of his pinky and ring finger on his right hand were missing, and hair was growing out of them. "What happened to your fingers?" I asked.

Owsley laughed dismissively. "I was a kid. But they grafted skin from my belly. That's why hairs grow." He lifted up his shirt and showed me a keloid scar next to his belly button. He was wearing bikini underwear.

Owsley wandered into the kitchen and opened the refrigerator.

I followed him. "Would you like something to eat or drink?" I offered, a little starstruck.

He took out the peanut butter jar and spooned a taste. "This is the only thing in your fridge I can eat."

"It's not *my* fridge. It's Perry's apartment. I have my own apartment, and you do not know what I like to eat."

"Then let's go to your apartment." He pinched my nipple and put his tongue in my mouth.

I stepped back. He was fast and tasted like peanut butter. I laughed. He smiled and cupped my breasts in his hands, then moved his hands down my back and played with my ass.

"Nice and round and tight, like a dancer. I studied ballet. Ballet is the best exercise, far superior to any sport."

I was delighted. "What? You?" He was so macho.

He pointed his toe and placed my hand on his calf. His leg was muscular. He took my other hand as if to lead me in a pas de deux but steered me toward the front door of the apartment.

Owsley spoke as we danced toward the door.

"Everyone should have a license to broadcast on the radio. In times of revolution, control of the airwaves is crucial. I have a first-class license, but a third-class license allows you to broadcast. Anyone who can read can get a third-class license. Are you interested?"

I answered him without hesitation. "Yes."

"I have the manual for the radio licensing exam in my vehicle."

Outside, it was a gorgeous California autumn afternoon. Owsley's white Valiant was parked right in front of the door. He opened the trunk where boxes of different sizes and contents were neatly arranged. He put his hand on my butt, drew me to him, and kissed me.

I looked into his hazel eyes and caught myself. Perry was my boyfriend, but I thought, fuck it, this is freedom time. Bear was a bigger boyfriend. I kissed him back.

He took a Murine bottle out of his inner pocket.

"Open your mouth and close your eyes, and you will get a big surprise."

For a moment I thought he was about to put eye drops in my mouth. Then I figured out it was liquid LSD.

"Just a taste now."

I tipped back my head and opened my mouth. "Lift up your tongue," he instructed and squeezed a drop into my mouth. We laughed together conspiratorially. I tingled with anticipation.

Acid gave me an alternative reality, and my vision was magical. The gold threads in Owsley's silk shirt shimmered around him, as if he were a king and we were characters in a holy pageant. The ground below my feet was soft and rolled with my movements. Berkeley was a protected realm, and we were sovereign.

Owsley leaned into the trunk, resting on his hip, shifting his weight from his leg, and spoke didactically: "There is nothing we cannot do."

He picked up a book bound in a commercial black cover. "This is the manual to prepare you for the broadcasting exam." He thumbed through the pages until he found what he was looking for. "Can you do this kind of calculation? This is an example of what's on the test." He held out the opened book with his finger pointing to a paragraph.

"This is algebra. I can do it," I said.

"I know you can pass the test, if you study."

"I'm good at that. Can I have the manual?"

"You'll have to return it. It's Melissa's. But you can share it. You can take the exam together."

"Who's Melissa?"

"She's my ole lady."

My jaw dropped. My mind was racing, peaking on acid. I saw the soul connection between Owsley and me. No one else mattered.

We went to my place where we made love until the sun came up. He ate a jar of my peanut butter and disappeared.

At Mother's in San Francisco, Owsley introduced me to Melissa. I felt subdued. She was sweet and friendly, with long brown hair and bright eyes, petite like me, and open, not the vicious sex siren I had dreaded.

"Do I know you?" I looked her in the eye. "You went to UC Berkeley?"

"Yes," Melissa said. "I majored in chemistry."

"That's not how I know you. The only science I took was physics for non-science majors because it was a requirement for graduation, but the teacher was Edward Teller."

Melissa winced. "Did you graduate?"

"Yes," I nodded, "but I almost failed physics."

Melissa waited for an explanation.

"I didn't go to lab."

"Was it a wet lab?"

"I don't know. I didn't go."

She laughed.

"No, it was a book report. That's what was so ironic! I was an English major. Did you live in the dorm?"

"I lived in the dorm before I moved in with Bear."

"I lived in the dorm before I moved off campus."

"We met in the dorm!" Melissa laughed and we hugged.

When I heard Pigpen sing "I went down to see a gypsy woman," I grabbed Owsley and led him to the dance floor.

A few weeks later, dressed for a costume party in a paisley net dress, I was delighted to run into Owsley outside the Trips Festival at the venerable old Longshoreman's Hall. He looked like a troubadour in his colorful ribboned shirt and tight jeans. A Merry Prankster in a Day-Glo skeleton suit and painted face danced before Bear and opened his mouth. Owsley took out his Murine bottle of pure liquid LSD. Drop, drop into his mouth. I opened my mouth. Drop, drop—yum!

Inside was a party as the Grateful Dead played. Owsley took me by the hand and danced with me across the floor where he introduced me to his friend Richard Alpert, the renowned Harvard associate of Timothy Leary and coauthor of *The Psychedelic Experience*, the definitive psychedelic textbook of the time. Richard was so handsome. I couldn't believe he was actually a dropout. He had short curly hair, a sparkle in his eyes, and a graceful manner. He spoke in a cultured Bostonian voice, even while shouting over the music.

We merged with the crowd, and Richard and I danced. We were suited as dance partners, performing hand-offs and spins without missing a beat, though he was tall and somewhat lanky and I was short, round, and sensuous. We moved together in time. I felt joy.

In the phantasmagorical lights, my LSD vision was clear and sharp. Owsley suddenly popped into my foreground. Under the strobe light his movements looked like the dance of a wooden puppet. He touched me, and we danced. We twirled around and I touched him as I turned and turned. Owsley spun with a balletic grace, always twisting his head and pointing, spotting for a fraction of a second. How many times could I spin without stopping—one hundred and eight? Somehow I knew there was a magic number, and the dance was an ancient ritual of devotion.

The band finished a song and Bear turned to me and asked, "Do you want Richard? You could have him, you know. Or do you want me?"

"I want you." I smiled. "You're the one for me," I said, and I meant it.

He was teasing me and touched my erogenous zones as we danced to a slower tune. He whispered in my ear, "Can I give you a ride home?"

He held my hand as we walked on Fillmore Street, away from the music. The cold air felt good. Suddenly we halted in front of an old bulbous car that looked like something in an R. Crumb cartoon. Bear extended his hand like an emcee introducing a boxing event.

"Rhoney, I present to you the Dreaded Dormammu, a 1949 Studebaker, the most reliable automobile ever produced in the United States!" I cared nothing about cars. This one was red and smelled of gas and oil. The passenger door didn't open from the outside.

I felt like a child as I climbed up onto the huge overstuffed front seat. "So dread Dormawho?"

"Dormammu," he enunciated. "The Dreaded Dormammu, the evil archenemy of Dr. Strange in the psychic realm. Marvel Comics."

I knew less about comic books than I knew about cars. My mother had always forbidden me to read them. "Oh," I said, "I thought you might have a Maserati."

He drove fast and well, and before I knew it, he had parked in front of my plain one-story building and turned off the car. As I shifted on the seat, I discovered I had been sitting on some sort of machine the size of a Cracker Jack box with a black leather casing.

"That's part of the Grateful Dead's new approach to sound. It's a condenser microphone. I'm making live recordings with a state-of-the-art sound system that captures the transformative moment of expression and creation with the audience who are also high on my LSD." He caught himself becoming overexcited, like Dr. Frankenstein sending up the kites, and paused. "Are you ready to show me your apartment?" With a flourish, I ushered him inside.

His passion made me passionate. After we made love, we sat naked in bed and talked for hours. "May I ask you a personal question?" he said.

"Yes," I replied.

"Do you use amphetamines?"

"No."

"Heroin?"

"No." I traced his beautiful lips with my tongue. He put a drop under his tongue and licked me. Owsley wanted more loving. By morning we could read each other's minds.

"I want you in my family. Your apartment would be perfect for pressing LSD into tabs. I'll teach you the whole process if you come aboard."

"Yes."

"Do you wish to think about it?"

"No." I was falling in love.

When he got ready to leave, he took a wad of hundred-dollar bills out of his vest pocket and gave them to me.

"Keep your apartment. We'll tab the LSD here."

While Owsley was away in LA with the Grateful Dead, I counted the days, but I wasn't the only one. The buzz was out. The Watts Acid Test had topped the charts. Now it was official. Owsley was the Grateful Dead soundman.

The windows of my apartment overlooked the street, and I saw Owsley and Richard Alpert approach. When I let them in, Richard smiled and put his arm around me, but Owsley carried a heavy machine to the kitchen counter and walked around the apartment, absorbed in his own considerations. Suddenly, he beckoned me toward him.

"I intend to press the LSD into tabs now. Richard is here because he wants the full experience." He held me close and put his tongue in my mouth.

"Yes," Richard said, "the entire process of making LSD is a sacred trip."

Richard Alpert Requests Nirvana

Nirvana (Sanskrit, निर्वाण): Extinction, a blowing out.

We blew our minds.

At Bear's house one day, I opened the door to the tall and handsome Richard Alpert. He could have just stepped out of *GQ* in his polo shirt, tan pants, and boat shoes with tassels. I took him to the kitchen where Bear was naked and totally engrossed in two large books open before him on the table: *Electrochemical Metallurgy* and *The Emerald Tablet of Hermes.* Richard and I waited for him to look up and acknowledge us.

"Is he reading those two books at the same time?" he asked.

"At least." I motioned for him to take a seat.

Richard sat and began talking with Owsley, who just added the conversation as a third object of his attention. "LSD is not enough to bring me to liberation and bliss. I always come back down into my thinking mind, this body, these clothes." Owsley looked up and uncrossed his legs, moving his balls out of the way with his hand.

Richard continued, "When I come down from LSD, I have lurid cravings and material desires. My visions are sexual and my mind is full of verbal conceits. I have a greater sense of specialness. My self-importance gets confirmation from LSD. This is not the consciousness I am after. I want to transcend my ego, go beyond words, beyond the boundaries of time and space. I cannot explain the plane of consciousness I reach high on LSD, and I cannot hold on to it. I'm going to India to look for an answer."

Owsley responded, "If you want to go to India, go to India, but you can transform yourself right here. Listen to music. Take more LSD." He pointed to the Murine bottle between his books.

Richard shook his head and gave up on his rap.

"Come, come," I comforted him and led him into the living room, pushed him onto the soft fabric couch, the perfect spot in the room for listening to balanced sound. "Let me play you some music." If I could not be at a live show, next best was listening to music at Bear's. He modified his home audio system by exchanging the components of the amp and preamp with precision parts he ordered from an aircraft manufacturer. He changed the type of cables and the wiring of the connectors. He had the best speakers—JBLs with the cones exposed. He even altered these, adding a subwoofer to increase the amplitude of the bass. His placement of the two tall speakers was calculated to optimize the quality of the sound. I pulled out an LP of the Bulgarian Women's Choir. I placed the record onto the turntable and dropped the needle.

"Jerry Garcia loves this," I told Richard.

"Jerry Garcia is a bodhisattva," he said.

High praise.

After the first song, I quickly switched to a recording of the Japanese *shakuhachi*, a type of bamboo flute—Zen flutists "blowing Zen." The music was so eerie that the musicians wore baskets over their heads to protect themselves from going crazy. During the Shogun years of political intrigue, revolutionaries pretending to be musicians wore the baskets on their heads to hide their weapons. At least, that's what it said on the jacket.

"That story appeals to the psychologist in me," he said.

"I thought it would appeal to the rebel in you," I joked. He didn't seem amused. I put away the Zen and picked up a new Ravi Shankar album and read from the cover:

> The ancient Vedic scriptures teach that there are two types of sound. One is a vibration of ether, the upper or purer air near the celestial realm. This sound is called Anahata Nad, or unstruck sound. Sought after by great enlightened yogis, it can only be heard by them. The sound of the universe is the vibration thought by some to be like the music of the spheres that the Greek Pythagoras described in the 6th century BC. The other sound, Ahata Nad, or struck sound, is the vibration of air in the lower atmosphere closer to the earth. It is any sound that we hear in nature or man-made sounds, musical and nonmusical.

Richard listened intently. "Very psychedelic," he commented. He became thoughtful. "I have a question for Merlin out there."

Richard stood up, took my hand, and led me back to the kitchen where the naked Merlin was still poring over his books.

Richard sat down across the table from Bear. "What if we intravenously inject pure crystalline LSD? That may be a way to make the psychedelic experience last. Certainly the purity of the experience will be perfect."

Owsley heard that. He saw his role as a psychedelic Prometheus, enabling mankind to choose to take a sacrament for transformation of mind and soul. His LSD was the purest. Purity of LSD was his raison d'être. He considered for a moment, then lifted his eyes to gaze at the two of us as if for the first time. "Inject directly into the blood stream, bypass the gut. Get a rush of LSD. I like it."

I was unprepared for Owsley's enthusiasm. Usually, if an idea weren't his, it couldn't be a good one.

"Let's do it next Saturday. I'll make the preparations."

Owsley invited a few friends who were eager to participate in the experiment. I reread *The Psychedelic Experience* to see how we could set up the environment for the most positive trip possible. The book said sexual visions are extremely frequent during the third bardo and erotic sexual orgies are often imagined: "You may wonder what sexual performance is expected of you . . . ."

What a funny book.

Early on Saturday afternoon, Owsley prepared the LSD for our purpose.

Placing a square of glassine paper on his Shimadzu precision scale, with his finger he tapped out crystalline LSD from a small brown bottle. He used a small glass funnel to pour homemade distilled water into another empty brown bottle, added the little pile of crystal from the glassine paper into the glass bottle, pushed on the rubber stopper, and mixed it by gently swirling the contents on the kitchen table.

At sunset, the group gathered—Melissa, three of Bear's cronies, Richard, and me. We had all eaten lightly in preparation for the psychedelic experience. Richard went first. He sat in a chair; Owsley tied a rubber tube around his biceps and injected the liquid into a vein inside his elbow. Richard said nothing, but his face said it all. His countenance was blissful, his mood was complete calm. He emanated love.

I was next and eagerly tied off my own arm, wiping the inside of my elbow with an alcohol swab. Bear probed a rising blue vein with a finger, the syringe in his other hand.

"How many micrograms are you giving me?" I asked, not hearing the answer as I was instantaneously transported to another realm.

All people disappeared. I, too, was invisible—bits of electric energy in the air, simply part of the space. The room had become a compartmentalized metal box. The walls were bare. The room was empty. Nothing was there. I uttered dulcet sounds rather than words and floated off into the atmosphere. I became dancing protoplasm. My boundaries dissolved. I felt fluid flowing through me, as if my body were ejaculating. I was hallucinating incestuous orgies and feeling my fertility. I was like the Earth and needed to be plowed.

Suddenly—commotion.

I reentered reality and heard, "I will murder Owsley."

One of Bear's friends, a biker from San Jose, was standing and pointing at him. He spoke in anger. "I'm going to get my gun and shoot Owsley."

Bear didn't say anything. He was shocked beyond words. We were all very high.

Richard said, "We cannot stop this impulse. We must play out this scene." He slowly approached the biker, who was breathing heavily. He put his hand gently on the man's shoulder and said quietly, "If you go outside, you will realize that we are the ones who love you. Slow down. Go easy. Stay with us."

Richard was brilliant. He got the guy settled on the floor and gathered the rest of us into a circle.

"Breathe in and out. Breathe in compassion. Breathe out loving-kindness. Connect to your loving awareness."

Joining hands, under Richard's skillful direction, we counted our breaths in rhythm, in and out, in and out. By the tenth breath, the biker broke down. He covered his face with his hands, apologizing profusely.

Owsley, being a true gentleman, forgave him, but the high was over. When our friends finally left, Owsley passed out on the couch. Richard and I danced to The Beatles' first album on the hi-fi.

"Do you think The Beatles mean it when they say, 'I'll always be true'?"

Richard said, "Yes. The emotion is so simple. It is liberating."

We sat outside under the stars, and Richard continued the conversation. "It is the same as loving. If I love, and you love, we create an atmosphere of love, and love connects us. It is not personal."

"It was your devotion to love that got us through tonight."

"We must tune in to love. Be love now." Richard paused momentarily. "Psychedelics alone cannot bring us there. Seva. Devotion."

For days, I was subdued. LSD had triggered an impulse of murder directed toward Owsley. Did Owsley cause this to happen? What was my role as his life companion and co-conspirator? I agreed with his mission to turn on the world, but I could see the danger. Some people could not handle psychedelic drugs.

Problem Child at Rancho Olompali

In May of 1966, Owsley invited me to accompany him to Olompali in northern Marin County where the Grateful Dead had rented a summer home on beautiful sloping grounds with clusters of old oak trees. The house was a rambling ranch in an elegant state of decay with many small interconnected rooms painted white and wallpapered years ago but now beginning to fade and flake. Every day was a new party.

Before sunset we began to trip. I found myself in a room with Jerry Garcia, hanging on to his threadbare deco armchair, the only piece of furniture in the house except for a few mattresses on the floor. I slid down and cuddled his cowboy boots. The walls were moving in and out; the ground was quicksand. Jerry was adrift in his own visions. I needed bodily contact to connect to myself. I needed to get off the floor.

Melissa was outside the window talking to a geek with heavy glasses. Their high-pitched laughter pierced my ears. Stop it, I wanted to shout. I needed music. Jerry held his guitar and picked some random licks. I spoke from an LSD haze.

"LSD changes perception. Music transcends the musician. You are a vehicle for communication."

Garcia stopped and stared at me.

"I practice," Garcia declared. "Anyone can do that."
That shut me up, and he returned to the guitar.

A girl came in and took my hand.

"Come outside," Girl said. She led me out the door into the moonlight. She was topless, her perfect breasts erect like a goddess. I pulled off my own shirt and let the gentle breeze caress me.

From out of the dark Bobby danced up to the stage. Garcia rambled out of the house. Phil was warming up, playing scales on his electric bass. His girlfriend was already dancing, her bare feet moving quickly, her long skirt rising as she twirled. Suddenly, there was music, intense, Phil pounding the bass as if he were a thunder god destroying the Earth.

I shouted, "Stop," but nobody heard me. I ran inside and fell on a mattress. Someone came and lay beside me. He played my body as if I were a musical instrument. It felt so good, I wanted more, but the music stopped. Whoever he was disappeared.

I stumbled outside. On the side of the hill, the kids had gathered. I listened to them. They complained that their parents did not take care of them. Two others said they had started smoking pot too young. The music boomed in the background.

"How old are you?" I asked.

One was fourteen; the other was twelve.

"Why don't you go into the pool?" I questioned.

"They're having sex in it," was the angry reply.

Bear was putting Sennheisers on microphone stands low to the stage. Girl was dancing wildly, her boobs bouncing up and down. She was smiling her mischievous Merry Prankster grin as she made her way toward the music.

"Aren't you coming?" she asked. We approached the stacks of speakers and stooped to feel the vibrations of the diaphragms. We moved with the hammering rhythm

of the percussion. It felt good. We put our heads so close
to Garcia's mic that the tone changed. If I could have put
my ear right up to the guitar strings, I would have done it.
I would have crawled into the amplifier. The loud music
drowned out the screaming of my childhood. I lost myself
and became the music.

The music stopped at dawn. All along the hill, sleeping
bags were on the ground and bodies were intertwined. In
the house every mattress was occupied.

Owsley advised us to take 270 micrograms of LSD
every five days. "LSD has a less toxic effect on human
biochemistry than most drugs at the dose we take. Every
drug is metabolized and eliminated, and adds a load to
the body's system. Always take the lowest dose to have
the therapeutic effect." He was probably taking it every
day, and there was no controlling the Grateful Dead.
He had estimated that LSD took five days to completely
leave the system.

Those summer nights were long and sensuous. Many
nights I hardly slept. Making love, listening to the sighs
and moans of everyone making love, I lost my identity.
I was nothing. This vision scared me. I felt replaceable.
Anyone could be me. The LSD experience of oneness
dominated, the consciousness that I was that and that I
was and we were indistinct from one another. I had no
ego sense of what I did, no sense that Rhoney swam in
the pool, washed the dishes, and danced. The conceptual
feeling that "I exist" disappeared. We lay under the stars
on the ground. The Earth felt like a cradle, and the
midnight blue sky glittered with the rays of thousands
of stars. I felt like a character living in Van Gogh's *Starry
Night*, part of the firmament. My self had shattered like an
exploding star, and I was afraid.

From a pay phone at Olompali, I called my psychiatrist in New York and got a referral to a shrink in San Francisco who had worked with psychedelics.

The Grateful Dead's managers, Danny and Rock, had business in the city, so I squeezed between the two of them in the front seat of the truck. The easy contact of our bodies felt good as I jostled up against them. When they dropped me off on California Street near the hospital, we made a plan to meet at the end of the day.

I walked up the stairs to the psychiatrist's office. The waiting room was small and I was alone. I rehearsed in my mind what I wanted to say. The door opened and the doctor showed me to his inner office. He was wearing a white shirt and a dark tie. He wore his thick hair in a duck cut. I spoke up without hesitation. I could hear the clock ticking.

"When I am high on LSD, I lose my self. I merge and lose my identity, and anyone can replace me."

"Tell me more about this loss of identity."

"When I have sex, I get a feeling of wholeness at the moment of orgasm. That is the only time the feeling of being replaceable goes away."

"Do you always have orgasms?"

"On acid, the trip is orgasmic. There's no difference between me and anyone else, and with sex, I merge. I become you . . ." I looked at this shrink in his suit and tie. "Not you."

I paused. What could he give me? Why was I here? Then I realized what I wanted. "LSD is still legal. Would you be willing to observe me in an LSD session?"

"I have no access to LSD."

"I can get the best acid, 99.9% pure. That's no problem."

"And where, my dear, can you acquire this LSD?" he asked much too eagerly.

My antenna went up. I could say from the street, but what value would therapy have if I weren't truthful?

"My lover makes the best LSD, named after him, 'Owsley acid.'"

"Is that so?"

He scribbled something in his notebook, then looked up at me.

"The psychiatric community is not all that certain LSD has any therapeutic value, now that LSD is the street drug of choice."

What a cop-out, I thought.

"Aren't you supposed to be investigating LSD?"

"Let's talk about you. Tell me more about what you feel."

"I feel that I'm nobody, that anyone could be me."

He looked at his watch. His eyes were hidden by dark framed glasses.

"Are you on LSD right now?" he asked.

I looked at him askance. "What do you mean?"

His voice took on a more menacing quality.

"I am very concerned about you. I believe you are in a vulnerable state." He was using my very words. Taking LSD made me vulnerable.

"In your best interests, I am recommending hospitalization. I can arrange to have you admitted now. Your parents have given me the authority. It's for your own good."

For your own good. That was what Father said when he spanked me with a belt. Automatically sensing danger, my body tensed, my muscles contracted, and my heart raced. I moved from a slouch to an erect position and focused my eyes on the doorknob, knowing I had to get away. I sprinted across the room, flung the door open, and bolted from the doctor's office. On the street, I put out my thumb to hitch a ride. Anywhere was better than there. The first car that stopped was a muscle car with automatic windows, and I jumped into the passenger seat.

"Thanks."

The man behind the wheel had a crew cut and was wearing shorts. When I got in, he pushed a button and closed the window. The air conditioning hummed.

"Where are you going, my dear?"

I took a breath and looked out the window. It was a rare sunny day in San Francisco. I leaned back in the comfortable seat, a luxury car like my dad's. My psychiatrist had betrayed my trust as a patient. My parents wanted to commit me.

"Away from that psychiatrist."

He drove to the top of Twin Peaks and stopped the car. The Summit Reservoir, at the top of Twin Peaks, was a San Francisco landmark. I had been there before. I was no innocent. I knew he had not taken me up there to look at the view of the Pacific Ocean.

I looked at his lap. He had taken his cock out of his shorts and was rubbing it up and down with his hand. He bent down and spit on it, wetting it with his saliva. My body tensed. I could give in, suck him off. Nobody would know; nobody would care. I pursed my lips, ready to bend down and suck his cock. It was thick, smooth and glistening, and the tip had a perfect ridge. I imagined my mouth forming a circle.

Suddenly, something in me snapped. My mouth was so dry I could not cry out, but I opened that door and flew out of that car. I ran down the trail. I knew my way and started the long walk back to rendezvous with Rock and Danny.

On our drive back to Marin, I told them what happened. Rock kept shaking his head. He drove with one arm out the window and one arm around me. With the window down, the wind made his straight hair tumble into his eyes. Danny held me close.

Rhoney the idiot ended treatment with Dr. Sidney Asshole. I had been exposed to Life Lesson 101, but I still didn't get it. I didn't trust LSD. I didn't trust myself. I turned to speed and fell further down the well of despair. I read in Robert Greenfield's *Timothy Leary: A Biography* that in 1966, one out of seven admissions to county psychiatric units were due to LSD-precipitated psychoses. I wonder how many of those were without patient consent.

That Sunday, on my regular call to Father, I asked him for a ticket home, and he readily agreed.

Owsley drove me to the San Francisco airport. "You can't go on this way," he admonished. We stopped at a motel for a quickie. Sex was still my passion. I could give up drugs but not sex. I needed more sex before I left.

We were lying in bed nude on top of each other. The room was dark; the windows bordered the ceiling. "Call Nick if you need help," Owsley offered. "He's a chemist, Jewish, like you, and he lives in New York."

"My parents live in the Westchester suburbs, not New York." I was bummed. Sex helped, but the high wore off.

"More pussy," he moaned.

"What will you do without Jewish pussy?" I asked and climbed up onto him again.

"You won't stay long in New York," he predicted.

My skin was yellow. I had no energy and slept all day. My mother was infuriated with me and barely spoke to me. When she did, she yelled, "Something's wrong with you. You're a loser!" My father was worried and dragged me to doctors for a diagnosis. I kept mum. I told no one of my drug use. How could a physician make a diagnosis if the patient does not disclose the correct history?

It was winter, 1966. I read the *New York Times* and saw that Ravi Shankar was playing Carnegie Hall. I was determined to go. I put on my hippest clothes, a long flowing skirt and a low-cut peasant top, and wrapped myself in a shawl. I sat in the audience and listened to the transforming music with other young people dressed as tastefully as me, but I had no energy, no passion. Even the heavenly sounds and the devotion of the audience could not inspire me. Even the sexy guys did not turn me on. I was lethargic, and when my dad picked me up, I collapsed even further. I lay down in the back seat of his big American car and pondered what I was doing. When we got home, my mother yelled some more.

I had been home almost two months and it was time to leave again. I called Nick and he drove to Westchester to get me. I took my clothes and jewelry, and whatever money I could find hidden in my mother's underwear drawers.

Nick lived in Brooklyn, on the top floor of his mother's brownstone, but his mother was cool. She had boyfriends. She bragged about Nick, "My boy, the chemist, follows in his dad's footsteps."

"Nick," I asked, "Does your mother know what kind of chemistry you do? Does she know about the drugs?"

He laughed. "If the narcs came here looking for me, Marcia would say, 'Nick, Nick who?'"

How different from my mother. I could be comfortable at Nick's. For days, I stayed in bed and listened to music. I didn't care what, as long as there was sound.

When I felt better I helped Nick's mom with the dishes.

"Has Nick performed cunnilingus on you?"

Marcia's voice was matter-of-fact and I, not knowing what "cunnilingus" meant, yet knowing she loved her son, answered enthusiastically, "Oh, yes, yes. Of course." We bonded. Marcia reminded me what it was like to be happy. The next time we did dishes, we both wore bikinis.

Nick's lab was in the warehouse district of Brooklyn. We walked the abandoned streets like we owned them. "We are commandos in the psychedelic army," Nick chanted, his round baby face glowing, his mouth twisting as he enunciated his words.

In front of a cyclone fence and a pile of bricks, Nick pulled out a bindle. "Try this." He put some powder in the palm of my hand, and I swallowed it.

Immediately, I felt nauseous and dizzy. I held on to Nick and groaned, "I think I'm going to throw up," and then threw up.

"I guess we need to purify it. It's usually impurities that induce nausea. Sorry. I thought you'd like it," Nick commented, holding me up.

"What is it?" I wiped my mouth with a tissue.

Nick laughed, "3,4-Methylenedioxymethamphetamine!"

"Fuck. I promised Owsley I wouldn't take speed."

"It's not speed. It has psychedelic characteristics."

Taking a psychedelic was my personal choice, but the government didn't see it that way. LSD became illegal on October 3, 1966. The underground chemists were manipulating a class of psychedelics—MDA, MMDA, MDMA—to stay one step ahead of the government's rampage on psychedelics. By changing one molecule on the compound, the name of the structure changed, but the psychoactivity remained. Nick's drug of choice was DMT, dimethyltryptamine. DMT was a powerful short-acting psychedelic with strong chemical similarities to hallucinogens found in nature like ayahuasca used by the shamans of indigenous cultures during vision quests.

"Trippy for tryptamine," I joked.

When we got back Nick's brownstone he wanted me to lie down in his bed on the third floor, but I insisted on helping Marcia set the table for dinner.

From left: Jerry Garcia, Melissa Cargill (wearing hat), and Owsley at Rancho Olompali

Timothy Leary Rocks Reality

Months passed. I was hired as a social worker in Harlem. The best part of the job was our afternoon meetings on the roof discussing cases and smoking pot. In April, Owsley called. He was coming to New York to meet Timothy Leary and invited me to join them.

"Is Melissa coming to New York with you?"

"Of course," he replied. He was making it clear: Melissa was number one, and if I wanted to be with him, I had to share him with Melissa.

"I can't just drop everything. I have a job," I said.

"Quit your job," he said. "It's time for you to come back to California. The psychedelic revolution needs you. I'll give you a job." He was good on the phone, too.

I met him at Richard Alpert's apartment on West 57th Street. He was alone.

"Where's Melissa?" I asked.

"At the Museum of Natural History. We're alone," Owsley replied, caressing, nibbling, exciting me.

The drapes were drawn and the only light came from Richard's white cat. She darted from one part of the modular couch to the other, then disappeared. Mattresses covered with Indian bedspreads were made up, but Bear took me down on an exquisite Persian rug on the parquet floor and made love to me, hushing me whenever I tried to speak. When we came, I moaned with pleasure and he yelped like a wild dog. Suddenly, the doorbell rang. We giggled like naughty children as we hurriedly put on our clothes.

Bear opened the door for Melissa, who wearily smiled and walked past us. I was afraid she might smell sex on me. I would have. But she went straight to the sofa and flopped down. Bear stood in front of her. "So how was New York?"

Melissa's eyes widened. "I love it, but I could never live here. My feet are killing me." It was her first visit to New York City.

"We can get insoles for you. And I know the coolest place to take you. I was there with my daddy when I was a little girl. You'll love it, but first I've got to shower and change."

The New York City parking angels were with us and we found a spot right on Third Avenue and Thirteenth Street. Kiehl's had been there since 1851, even before the current nineteenth-century, three-story brick building had been built. As we approached the storefront window with its collection of remedies and antique bottles with handwritten labels, Owsley's delight was palpable. I held open the double doors and ushered in my openmouthed friends. A woman in a clean white lab coat smiled at us from behind a glass and walnut display case. Owsley spoke to her for a minute before she summoned Aaron Morse, the owner and proprietor, who appeared from the back room. Owsley asked so many informed questions that Aaron invited us to follow him behind the curtain. Hanging from the ceiling was a vintage single-seat airplane above his collection of vintage cars and motorcycles. Owsley told Aaron that the Hell's Angels had gifted him with a Harley Davidson. This started another conversation. It was remarkable how much they had in common.

Suddenly, something caught Bear's eye. He strode over to a curved glass display case of antique pharmacy bottles. Aaron opened it and Owsley made a point to use his disfigured right hand to deftly pick up a solid-based amber glass dram bottle. His club hand was claw-like in its dysfunction. Aaron smiled as he realized he was being tested.

He spoke, "Like the hand-ground glass stoppers, do we?"

"Yes, we do."

"Take it with my compliments."

That was the icebreaker, and Bear started buying.

Melissa and I wandered over to a perfumery area. Owsley had promised to customize perfumes for us, and Kiehl's specialized in perfumes made from pure oils. We sniffed and sniffed like little girls dreaming of romance. I liked French lilac, which was different from plain lilac, less flowery.

Owsley appeared and thrust an open bottle under my nose. Instantly feeling dizzy, I gagged, making a guttural sound to stop myself from puking. Melissa had the same reaction.

"Civet," he grinned. "Extract from the anal glands of a cat, acts like a fixative, preserves the perfume, but smells like shit. Musk is another fixative—comes from the umbilicus of domestic deer in the Himalayas. The name is borrowed from the Sanskrit word for scrotum."

Melissa and I laughed. Owsley was pleased.

He put an essence on my wrist. I bent close to the drop of oil, expecting sweetness, but the scent was original.

"What is it?"

"Chypre. Interesting, wouldn't you say? Has a woodsy smell, like you," Owsley whispered, stroking my butt.

I was definitely buying chypre.

Owsley chose ylang-ylang for Melissa.

"This is the fragrance of all fragrances. That is the meaning of 'ylang-ylang,'" Owsley explained.

I didn't like the smell. It was sickly sweet to me.

He waved a brown glass bottle with a rectangular stopper under my nose. Patchouli. He didn't even have to pull the stopper for me to recognize the scent. We smelled all the different scents of patchouli, discerning the differences, and with our input, he selected several patchouli essences.

"Patchouli definitely smells like marijuana," I told him.

"Hogwash. Only cops think so."

Exactly, I thought.

Melissa and I looked at each other. We knew he wore patchouli to attract other chicks. As if we weren't enough.

Owsley bought patchouli, the civet, the musk, and other ingredients for making perfumes, as well as materials to make skin lotions. He was developing a body lotion, Barely Burn Bear Brand, and was aiming for the most uniform suspension, all fluid with no solid globules. Aaron showed him different varieties of lanolin. He bought a lamb, a sheep, and a goat lanolin.

In the back of the back room was the laboratory, a definite point of interest for us. Aaron proudly showed us the distillation setup. Owsley praised the glassware, the rounded bevels, the variety of flasks, and the overall compactness and efficiency. As he spoke, he put his arm around Melissa, as I stood several feet away listening to the rain hit the pavement on Third Avenue.

"What would be the scent of rain?" I wondered out loud, "sharp but smooth."

"Electric," Owsley quickly responded. He took something out of his vest pocket. He and Aaron walked away, but soon were back with smiles on their faces.

"We'll make a scent and call it 'Rain,'" Aaron promised.

"Wait till the Grateful Dead come to New York City," Owsley exclaimed. "They'll love this place."

"I'll send a limo to pick them up," Aaron commented, excited about meeting the Grateful Dead.

Owsley spent another hour packing all the loot in the trunk of the car. He was compulsive about orderliness. The entire trunk of the rental car was full of bottles wrapped in brown paper, packed in cardboard boxes, as we headed to Millbrook to meet Timothy Leary.

We arrived at Millbrook late, of course. We drove up a long graveled driveway to a circle in front of a big old Victorian house, hardly visible in the dark, except for its steeple and painted facade. Millbrook had once been the country estate of the Andrew Mellon family, a banking family from Pittsburgh, and one of their descendants, Billy Hitchcock, had invited Timothy Leary to live there and continue the LSD experimentation he had started at Harvard. Billy had a sister, Peggy, who was into the Grateful Dead and in love with Leary. Neither heir nor heiress was present.

Owsley was speaking to Richard Alpert, who was present, as ever. "I'll see Billy in New York, but where is Tim?"

Richard seemed agitated. Rosemary and Tim had secluded themselves in the tower and did not want to be disturbed. Melissa looked perplexed. This was not the greeting she had expected. To us, Owsley's meeting with Timothy Leary was a headline event—the meeting of the East and West Coast psychedelic gurus. I expected to take LSD with the authors of *The Psychedelic Experience* and blow my mind.

"There are too many people here for the amount of space," Richard informed us. "Timothy invited Bill Haines, a guru who was tossed out of an ashram for using LSD. You can't turn down an LSD refugee. Who knew his sixty-five devotees would follow him? Rosemary is freaking out. The house has so few bedrooms with baths."

Owsley's eyebrows met. "What about us? Where's Tim?"

Richard pointed to a winding stairway and walked in the opposite direction, saying, "I'm going to meditate." We followed Owsley. There were bodies everywhere, even in a broom closet. We climbed the winding tower stairs to the solid oak door at the top. The self-styled icon appeared grinning with a martini in his hand; in his gauzy white Indian garb, he looked nothing like a former Harvard professor.

"Come on in. Rosemary can't deal with so many people," Timothy said, careful not to spill the martini as he closed the door behind us.

Rosemary was sitting on silk cushions by a long glass table. She too was floating a green olive in the proper glass. Rosemary was sinewy and long in a diaphanous rose outfit, and her thick, straight blonde hair was cut in an even style, the same length all around.

What's this? I wondered. Alcohol, not hallucinogens? I worried that Owsley would say something against alcohol and true to form, he did.

"Alcohol kills. I know firsthand. My father was an alcoholic. He died at a young age. He was dead before he died."

"Wasn't LSD used to treat alcoholism?" I asked as a way of joining the conversation.

"Yes, in the very earliest experimentation with LSD," Tim replied. After all, he was an academic, he knew the research.

Tim spoke in his mannered voice to Owsley, "Have you forgotten I'm Irish? I have the gift of gab and its accouterments." He raised his glass in a toast.

"You need to take more acid," Owsley declared.

Leary changed the topic and said the best thing possible. "In the refrigerator, we have T-bone and Porterhouse steaks, compliments of the tune-in, turn-on, drop-out road show."

That's all Tim had to say. Owsley's face lit up. "Meat!" he exclaimed as he dashed down the stairs to the kitchen.

By the time the rest of us got there, Bear was searing a sixteen-ounce Porterhouse in a black iron skillet over a front burner on high heat and giving Bill Haines, the vegetarian guru, an earful.

"The reason you're so fat is you eat excess carbohydrates."

Haines's followers gasped as the progenitor of the Northern Californian psychedelic revolution stabbed the purple, bloody steak with his fork and devoured it like a wolf, chewing on the bone with his teeth. Owsley never had the guru mindset; nor did he ever covet being any group's leader. He couldn't care less if you liked him. He wanted people to think independently.

Leary sipped his cocktail and declined Owsley's offering from the Murine bottle, but I opened my mouth for a big surprise as I sat on the floor in the cross-legged position of a dancer at rest.

"LSD is just a tool for transformation. We need more people on the bandwagon. Critical mass. That is my vision. The Grateful Dead are part of the equation—the audience, you too," ranted Bear, just warming up.

"I call it the feedback loop," he explained to Tim. "If the band hears themselves perform, they complete the loop."

Tim and Rosemary took their martini pitcher upstairs. Bear followed them, his rap unfinished. "Like an amoeboid loop. . ."

"Like bearing witness," I interrupted. "It's a major

concept in religion, on the path to enlightenment or ecstasy." I was already high. Owsley acid came on quickly.

Again Owsley offered his bottle of LSD to Tim, but he seemed more tuned in to Rosemary than to us, more turned on by alcohol than by psychedelics, and he dropped out of our greatly anticipated party. It was not happening. The hippies downstairs were more hospitable than the East Coast King and Queen of Hallucinogens. We left them to themselves and went back downstairs.

Owsley handed out tabs of LSD and STP and we danced, a wave of bodies moving in unison, coming together and reforming, ankle bells jingling. Males and females looked the same, wearing dresses as if they were pilgrims in India, moving in one sensual flow. Some older person said, "You don't see young people that beautiful any more." The Millbrook mansion was a mixture of old grandeur and disrepair. The wallpaper was peeling and the fireplace was bare, but the solid dark wood trim was stately. Outside on the grounds and in small structures more hippies were hanging out like anima and animus spirits in the landscape, wandering around the gardens, posing on the stone bridges. A large stone gatehouse was surrounded by topiaries. At dawn, we gathered around a heavy metal bell that was set in a cage in front of the house. The sun had not yet come up, and the light was dim. The painted mural on the facade looked like a Buddha in gaudy colors.

We were peaking on LSD, waiting for the sun as we accepted that Tim, Richard, and Ralph Metzner, the East Coast academics, were not joining us.

Melissa said, "Chalk it up to the difference between East Coast and West Coast. We make the purest acid, not rules on how to take it."

I said nothing. Was I East Coast? Was I West Coast?

Owsley picked up a hammer and, assuming it was there for the purpose, clanged it solidly on the bell. It rang so loudly, it shattered the remains of the night. Ralph appeared in his pajamas, running out of the house and down the steps screaming, "Stop! Stop that!" His hands were over his ears. He was in a rage. Furiously, he disappeared back into the slumbering castle as Bear quietly dropped the hammer. This was not community.

"What an angry little hornet of a man," Melissa hissed.

"Connection doesn't always happen."

"Sobering."

"What's that?" Owsley joked. We made our excuses and prepared to leave. We had intended to return to the city in a caravan with Richard Alpert, but we weren't going to sleep anytime soon. The Jefferson Airplane had a gig that night at the Café Au Go Go. Bear had new electronics for Jack Casady's bass and wanted to be there to help set up their sound system. Melissa was thrilled that we were leaving Millbrook and going to the Airplane's gig.

We took off without directions, still very high on acid and promptly got lost. We had arrived in the dark and nothing looked the same going in the opposite direction. Melissa, sitting in the front seat next to Owsley, pointed with her finger at a cop car and told Owsley to stop. She wanted to ask the policeman for directions. Was she crazy? She turned to me. "I was taught to always ask a policeman for help."

Owsley politely asked, "How do I get to the Taconic?" The cop was on the other side of the country road, and he got out of the police car to answer Owsley. I was seething! Were those two asking for trouble? But the cop gave us the directions. "Make a left turn, then another left turn.

Follow the curve, bear left, and that will take you to the
Taconic." He got back in his car, and I sighed with relief.

We started laughing. "No left turn unstoned," we
chanted in unison. "No stone left unturned." We thought
we were home free until we realized the cop was following
us. Our laughter was replaced by tense silence as we
wound along the unfamiliar country roads with the cop
car behind us. Owsley became so nervous with the cop in
his rearview mirror, he forgot to signal on the last left turn.
Instantly, we heard the shrill of the siren, the red light on
top of the patrol car flashing and whirling.

Melissa apologized for her mistake. "I forgot our current
status. Would a coyote help a lost roadrunner?" I thought,
did she really say that? I could hardly wrap my head around
what was going on as I sat awash in the cop's floodlight.

Owsley was fiddling with his shirt, rearranging his vest.
"There's nothing anyone can do now. We're screwed."

My ears were hurting, still ringing from the siren.
Through the window I watched the cop approach the car.
Owsley rolled down the window. He only rented cars with
manual windows. He could not hear what the cop was
saying and had to ask the cop to repeat himself. I was sure
we were arousing suspicion. We had long hair, we smelled
weird, and we were less than five miles from Millbrook.

Melissa, now silent, looked like a rural California girl,
but I was wearing a minidress with a black net midsection
that showed my belly button. I did not look like a good girl.

"Is there a problem, officer?" Bear asked.

"Failure to signal. May I see your driver's license and
vehicle registration?"

While Melissa searched the glove compartment, Owsley
fumbled in his vest pocket, looking for his driver's license.
Something fell out of his pocket, and he picked it up with his

mutilated fingers. The cop became suspicious and ordered Owsley to get out of the car and hand over the keys.

I jumped out of the car to support him. "What right do you have to search our car? We're just trying to get to the Taconic Parkway. That's all we're doing!" I hoped I was using a placating tone, but the cop ignored me; he was exploring the trunk for illegal drugs.

The car trunk was small and packed to the gills in the most functional array. Owsley was known for his ability to hide contraband and to meticulously pack so that anyone but he had a nightmare unpacking.

The cop did a double take as his flashlight beamed across the neat rows of packages, bags, and bottles. Maybe he was thinking that everything we had was a drug. Maybe he'd miss the real drugs for the perfumes.

He pointed angrily at Owsley and me. "Get in the car and stay there." He was the same age as us, but he had the military crew cut and all that went with it.

Owsley got in the driver's seat and turned the mirror to watch him, but the trunk lid was up. Suddenly I went from fight to flight; I could smell my fear.

The cop came to Owsley's window with one of the large brown bottles. "Can you tell me the contents, please?"

I burst into laughter out of fear and frustration. It was a sample of Barely Burn Bear Brand, Owsley's natural concoction for the benefit of the skin. It was a tongue twister, not a mind bender.

I opened the back door and got out of the car. I defiantly placed my hands on my hips. "We're not doing anything wrong," I told the cop. "You're the one who's wrong. That's skin oil."

Now the cop was angry. "Get in the car." I got back in the car. I wanted to cry. Now a small amber bottle became the object of his attention. Owsley was freaked out. The bottle was a rare example of handblown glass, the gift from the owner of Kiehl's.

The cop had removed the ground-glass stopper and was smelling the contents. "You are all under arrest. Follow me to the police station."

He did not call for backup; he did not handcuff us. We dutifully pulled out behind him and followed him. At the Duchess County police station, the interrogation continued with questions randomly fired at us.

"Do you know Timothy Leary?"

"Where are you coming from?"

"What drugs are you carrying?"

Owsley said, "We have the right to remain silent until we speak to a lawyer."

The cops ignored him. One cop, the one who had busted us, questioned me incessantly. He had it in for me.

"Where were you going? What were you doing? Do you sell drugs? Is he your husband?"

I answered question after question, seated on a metal folding chair under the fluorescent glaring light of the holding area. How long would this go on? What was his authority? Why were his rules better than mine? I was harming no one. Using LSD was my personal choice.

The cop stood over me, contemptuous. "You should be ashamed of yourself. Think how your parents would feel if they could see you now."

"How dare you talk to me this way!" I raised my hand as if to slap him in the face, and he grabbed my wrists. I lifted my knee and slammed him in the balls.

"You dirty hippie," he yelped and let go of my wrists.

Finally, the police let us each make our calls, and Owsley phoned Al Matthews in Los Angeles who had contacts with the famous Manhattan lawyers F. Lee Bailey and Henry Rothblatt. They agreed to take on the case and promised to post bail before evening so we wouldn't have to spend the entire night in jail. I phoned my parents, but no one answered.

Melissa and I were separated from Owsley and brought into a room for fingerprinting by a severe matron in a drab gray uniform. Melissa was scared the matron would strip search us, but she only made us get nude and weighed us. I wondered if Melissa had the key to Owsley's safe deposit box hidden in her pussy. While we waited in a cell with bunk cots and a toilet in the middle of the floor, Melissa and I exchanged life stories.

She grew up in a poor family in the San Joaquin Valley. She told me her family picked crops when she was a baby and brought her to the fields in a basket, that she had learned to drive a tractor before she drove a car. I told her I had been busted before—once for shoplifting and once for loitering, profanity in public, and kicking a cop in the balls.

"Rhoney," Melissa scolded, "You are incorrigible." Finally, she was smiling. "We have each other," she cried, and we hugged.

We made our way back to Manhattan, stopped at our new lawyer Henry Rothblatt's posh office in a brownstone on West End Avenue. He told us the police claimed they found drugs in plain view when they opened the trunk and that we had been charged with possession of illegal drugs. Later I learned the cops had found the key to the safe deposit box in the rental car but they never matched the key to the lock. Bear used his underground banking connections to empty the box and move the money to a Bahamian bank.

I called my parents again; my mother answered. I said, "Hello, Mommy."

She screamed, "I have no daughter," and hung up. News of my arrest was on the front page of *The Daily Argus*, the local newspaper my mother read every day. According to my younger brother, my mother had opened the newspaper, read the headline, "LOCAL GIRL ARRESTED WITH LSD KING," shrieked, had run to her bedroom, and stayed there for hours.

Owsley said, "We're getting the fuck out of here. We're on the next plane back to California."

He looked at Melissa and me. "Let's go home."

We were family.

The Instrument of Grace

Bear's brick house, on Valley Street in Berkeley, built by the Fox brothers, was big enough for all of us to feel comfortable. It resembled a whimsical storybook house, a Hobbit house with a steep gable roof of wooden shakes, a cylindrical chimney, sloping sides, and oddly shaped stained-glass windows. A cobblestone walkway led to the front door set in an archway. Inside were high ceilings, wooden beams, and stucco nooks like adobe altars. Bear said we wouldn't be there long. He was preparing to leave for his secret lab to make more LSD and invited me to assist him. He said he would pay me weekly. I loved the idea.

"You catch on quickly. You're a Virgo." He looked up from the newspaper and laughed. "You'll have no problem sticking to my rules on cleanliness and order."

"But what will I do?"

"Wash glassware. Assemble the apparatus. It's complex. Each procedure requires a different glassware setup." Each flask Owsley used met a special need. The glassware was built by Hank, a master scientific glassblower in Berkeley, specifically for Owsley according to his specifications. As with all the vendors he contacted as head of Bear Research, the company he had formed to do his business, he had become friends with Hank and his family. His sons came with us to Grateful Dead shows. Hank supplied ordinary glassware to scientific labs, but the designs he made for Owsley were unique.

"For example," he continued, "evaporation requires a
flask, an evaporating tube, and a collections vessel, and all
these must be securely connected with greased ground-
glass stoppers."

"I can do it."

"Many of the chemicals we use are highly volatile and
flammable; others are photosensitive or anhydrous and
require special handling."

"I can learn the names of the chemicals and their
properties."

"That's physical chemistry—the hardest of all
chemistries."

"I'll memorize. I can do that."

"Learn the vocabulary," he advised. "That's the
first step in mastering any discipline. Each field has a
vocabulary. If you learn the vocabulary, you can acquire
the material."

"When do we start?" I quipped, sashaying up to him.

There was a problem. Melissa had stashed 500 grams of
lysergic acid monohydrate powder in a safe deposit box and
had forgotten the name she used to open the box. Without
the starting material, there was nothing to do. We could not
move forward. It was as simple as that. Bob Thomas, Willy,
Bear, and I gathered in the living room in front of the fire.
We all wanted to help Melissa remember. Bear called out
names: "Berdie, Girl, Lavender, Bella, Iridesca," and Melissa
shook her head, "No, no, no, no."

I said, "If you gave yourself the name, you will
remember it. Think carefully." But I was no help. Melissa
simply could not remember.

Bear was desperate and got a recommendation over
the phone for a local hypnotist who promptly materialized
on our doorstep. What a sleazebag: a sixty-year-old

wearing tight pants and too much Brylcreem in his butch cut. He was much too solicitous of Melissa and sat down too close to her in front of the fireplace.

"Look into the fire," he commanded in an unctuous voice. "Watch the flames rise and fall. Clear your mind. Let go!"

I was getting hypnotized instead of Melissa. She was giggling and basking in the attention. The session was a failure.

He said, "Your friends are a distraction. I must be alone with you. Where can we be alone?"

Bear responded, "Upstairs, in the bedroom."

"Come, Melissa, come with me." The hypnotist put his hand on Melissa's elbow and propelled her toward the stairs.

"Missy," she cried. "Missy's the name I used on the safe deposit box. Missy Stanley."

"Now," Bear said, "we can begin. Pack your bags. Be ready to move when I say so."

He was checking the astrological forecast for the best time to start the LSD synthesis. He was very into the sacred nature of making LSD, and as much as he could, controlled the conditions. This was his personal ritual and not public.

At the very last moment, he informed us of the time and place. Aquarius was the astrological sign. Denver was our destination. I was glad the time was now, but confused that Denver, a relatively large city, was the location of our clandestine LSD lab. Bear did not explain, and I did not ask any more questions.

Owsley, Melissa, and I flew from San Francisco to Denver at night, and I could see nothing but stars in the sky, no Rocky Mountains. Owsley's lab protégée, Tim, met us at the Denver Airport in a beat-up old van. He was tall and lanky with greasy hair and Clark Kent glasses with thick lenses. He was wearing a plaid shirt and work boots, cords belted at the waist like a Wild West nerd.

First stop was the drice plant. "Drice" was Bear's word for "dry ice." He insisted that we use his lingo, too. Making LSD required hundreds of blocks of dry ice. We used drice as a coolant because LSD and its derivatives are heat labile, meaning they decompose with a rise in temperature. I paid attention to the details. The drice plant was open twenty-four hours. Tim backed up to the loading dock and Owsley went in. Fifteen minutes later he came out smiling.

"No problemo." He had made friends with the night clerk. "We'll load up."

I teetered under the weight of a 50-pound block of drice wrapped in brown paper, smoking in my hands. Not a very challenging task, I ruminated.

Tim headed toward our new home. Within minutes, he had driven from an industrial to a residential neighborhood, a suburban subdivision. The houses were large with wide front lawns, but they all looked the same.

He pulled into the driveway of a bilevel house with a garage. "We unload here."

We entered the house through the garage and carried in the drice. The lab was very quiet, almost hushed except for the whir of the vacuum pumps, which we used in the last step of the synthesis. Before we had arrived, Tim had cut down 110-gallon drums to hold the three 72-liter condensing flasks. The "pot" of each flash evaporator, where the boiling took place, was a modified 22-liter flask. The huge vacuum pumps accommodated Owsley's new cooling process at the final crystallization stage. Lysergic acid compounds begin to decompose if heated above room temperature; nevertheless, at several stages in the procedure to evaporate the solvents, we had to subject the LSD compounds to heat. Owsley's research had accumulated evidence that not only was it necessary to change solvents, stripping off one and adding another, but also that vacuum evaporation reduced the air pressure, which caused the solvents to boil at lower temperatures. If evaporation of the solvents was done under vacuum, we could even use cold water as a heat source for the flask of boiling solvent. This process saved the LSD from too much exposure to heat. The product was purer, the yield higher.

It was amazing how the man could educate himself from those chemistry tomes he was always schlepping around. He did not invent the procedure of flash evaporation and its application in making LSD. The procedure was well known to straight chemists who worked with ergot alkaloids, such as Albert Hofmann, who had discovered the psychedelic properties of LSD on April 19, 1943. But it wasn't explained clearly in their patents and articles. Bear was able to understand and interpret what the academic chemists reported. He enjoyed feeding

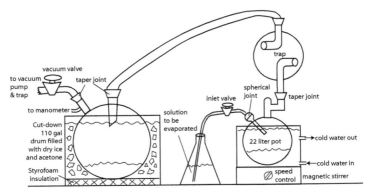

Tim Scully's flash evaporator from the 1967 Denver lab   © *Tim Scully*

my interest in learning the science and chemistry of our experimentation. He taught me a lot and convinced me that LSD had accelerated my learning curve.

He heaved a trunk of books into our new place, bending under its weight, and Melissa and I followed him, Tim helping us with our luggage. We all went down to the basement to see the lab.

"I see the drums are ready for the first run, Tim."

"Yup."

Owsley switched on a yellow light. "We'll add the drice and dilute with acetone," he declared.

I didn't dare ask why. I was intimidated by Owsley's professionalism and humbled that I was getting paid as an equal member of the crew. I wondered what I would be doing, but succeeded in keeping my mouth shut until I knew more.

"You and Melissa can dilute the drice with acetone. This will effectively provide more cooling power than the drice alone. The condenser must be very cold—minus 78 degrees centigrade. We use the metric system," Owsley instructed. "We'll get started in the morning." He turned off the lights.

Upstairs the house had three small box-shaped bedrooms and was carpeted with "ticky tack" materials, as if it were the prototype for the Malvina Reynolds' song, "Little Boxes"—a political satire about conformist values and tract housing in suburbia. Melissa lugged her trunk into the master bedroom and Owsley followed her, making it clear who was bedding whom. Tim and I had our own bedrooms.

We had special tapes that the bands had given us to use while we were making the LSD. Owsley put on the Grateful Dead. Tim had wired together a preamp and amp and assembled bass speakers that Phil had once tried for his guitar. I gave Tim a hug and told him, "The system you set up sounds great." He was so tall, he had to bend at the waist to reach me. Behind the glasses, his eyes were unwavering and full of love.

My first morning in Denver, sunlight woke me. Melissa was in the kitchen making tea, and Owsley was sitting nude at the table thumbing through a phone directory.

"Now," Owsley said, "we need to find a butcher. Colorado is known for its beef, and we will eat like kings." He looked through the yellow pages and found a butcher on Colfax Avenue. He picked up the phone and ordered chuck steaks.

"Chuck, isn't that the cheapest cut? Why didn't you order fillet mignon, the connoisseurs' choice?" I asked.

"I would never buy fillet mignon," Owsley disdainfully answered me. He put a French accent on the words. "Fillet mignon has little fat, and although it may be soft to chew, it is tasteless. I can feed a whole family of six with what two fillets would cost me. This is another example of mindless spin dictating taste. To say fillet mignon is the best cut of meat is pure drivel."

"Well, that's what I was taught growing up. At home, the meat had to be kosher, and if we went to a restaurant, we ordered fillet mignon."

"Rhoney, ride the bicycle to the butcher's and pick up the meat. I'll prove to you what's right." He handed me a hundred-dollar bill. "Go!"

Inside the garage was an old Schwinn with three gears and a big basket in the front. I opened the garage door. No one around. Anyway, what would they see? All that was visible was a routine garage with a workshop. I rode out onto the streets feeling like a normal young girl taking a morning jaunt in suburban Denver, backed by the Rocky Mountains.

When I returned from my butcher errand, Owsley seared the meat over a high flame and cooked it quickly.

"The only way to eat meat is blood rare. What's the sense of eating anything after you've cooked out all the nutrients?"

Bear called his diet the "primitive man's diet," and he attacked his blood-rare steak like a primitive man, stabbing the meat with a knife and bringing the knife to his mouth, au jus too much. I used a knife and fork.

"Unnecessary," Bear decried, watching me.

I put a slice of his chuck in my mouth. The texture was satisfying and the flavor delicious. Owsley picked up a bottle of Pickapeppa sauce and poured some on the meat, cut a piece, and held it to my mouth. "This is good for variety. You may have a preference in sauces, but unless I make my own, I like this brand."

I liked the Jamaican flavor, pungent and strong, and applied it like Bear, who wasn't done with his rap.

"Generally I prefer meat without any sauce, in its natural juices. When you don't cook meat with salt, the juices bathe the meat in flavor instead of bleeding out into the pan. It's like osmosis. In a cell, salt and other electrolytes draw out the fluid to set up an equilibrium. We want the juices to stay in the meat. We don't want equilibrium in a frying pan." He looked pleased.

We finished eating and went down to the basement lab.

Making LSD

Owsley instructed me in the basics of LSD manufacture. "Yellow light emits very little visible or UV light. That is why we change all the light bulbs to bug lights. LSD starts to decompose when exposed to visible or UV light."

We were all wearing our new wired-rimmed glasses, like John Lennon. We looked more buglike in the bug lights.

Owsley explained we needed to take care, even when the tasks appeared mundane, like washing and drying the glassware.

"The whole process is only as strong as the weakest point," he added, referring to the chemical protocol.

Melissa was the designated expert, and it was her job to teach me. We wore masks, paper throwaway smocks, and expensive rubber gloves with grips so we would not drop the goo
 necked flasks. Alongside the stainless steel sinks was a plastic squirt bottle of acetone.

Melissa took a washed beaker, squirted acetone on it, and held it up for inspection.

"See how clean! Look. The beaker is dry. Every piece of glassware must have a final rinse of acetone."

"Oh, that acetone smells terrible. Anything that smells that bad can't be good for you."

"Acetone smells bad but the flasks are glad," Melissa responded. She blasted the beaker with compressed air. "This hastens the drying process." She examined the glassware; if it were wet or there were any streaks or spots, it would come back for a do-over.

We fell into a routine: eat, sleep, and work.

We usually worked at night, and for this phase of the synthesis, columns clamped to rods were setup. Tim was in charge of packing them because he was tallest. The process is called column chromatography, or affinity chromatography, because the desired LSD—the iso-LSD—and the impurities have different affinities for the alumina adsorbent and separate out at different rates, or affinities, as they travel down the column. According to Bear, the trick was to get the mother liquor down the

column without it breaking off into crystals along
the way.

When Owsley first started making LSD, he did not use
column chromatography to purify the acid. He used vacuum
desiccation. He turned off all the lights and dried the LSD
in a vacuum desiccator, basing his decision to use the
vacuum on the principle that vacuum desiccation speeded
up evaporation. The more solvent he pulled out of the LSD
and the quicker he did it, the purer the product and the less
decomposition. But to open the lid of the desiccator, he had
to let in a gas, and in the dark, he let dry nitrogen into the
vacuum desiccator. When he opened the lid, flashes of white
light flooded his eyes. The pressure change in the chamber
caused a mechanical disruption, and the acid decomposed.
Owsley had discovered a property of LSD now known as
the Owsley effect, or piezoluminescence, which although
brilliant is indicative of stress on the LSD. He changed to
column chromatography at this stage, and he spread the
word to the other underground chemists. He also stopped
breaking up the crystals while they were in the mother
liquor because he saw the same telltale lightning flashes.
Chromatography yielded even more pure product for the
amount of starting material than his previous synthesis
process, but it was a slow, arduous process, and none of us
were tall enough to help Tim.

I was in charge of the music. Owsley had brought a
library of tapes and cassettes to Denver, but with only a
reel-to-reel recorder, a cassette player, and Tim's rig, we did
not have a full system. My favorite tape for making LSD
was a long rendition of "For What It's Worth," performed
by Buffalo Springfield: "Hey people, what's that sound?
Everybody look what's going down." We also had a special
tape from Blue Cheer, the band named after Blue Cheer

LSD, blue 270 microgram tabs of pure Owsley acid. The best thing about their music was the power. Blue Cheer had the reputation of playing so loud they blew out studio monitors. When we were running loud machinery like the vacuum pumps, nothing was better than Blue Cheer to drown out the sound of illicit activity.

Once the columns were packed with alumina and wetted with the eluting solvent, chloroform, we were ready to start the purification of LSD. The lab was bathed in yellow light, softening the room. Holding a goosenecked flask, Owsley poured the mother liquor down the column. In the background, the vacuum pump pounded and the music roared.

As the solution of LSD flowed down the column and dispersed in the alumina, I was awed by the multicolored rivers of light.

"'Legs' is the proper nomenclature," Bear said and snapped on a UV light to follow the bands as they travelled down the chromatography column. "This must be used sparingly," he declared, waving the wand.

"Look at that dark green band! Breathtaking!" I felt transported, as if I were watching flashes of bright stars in a celestial dome.

"Impurities," he responded.

I was entranced: the deepest of colors, the most vibrant—impurities!

The first isolate to come out of the column was the LSD. I was so excited, I wanted to taste it, but Owsley said it was the LSD base and still had chloroform in it.

I had seen the yellow hazard label on the bottle of chloroform and read the warnings.

"Chloroform—a most toxic chemical—I can only imagine its horrible taste."

Owsley's face scrunched up. "Chloroform actually tastes sweet and pungent, but it is a poison." He carefully stooped, held the collection vessel under the column, and opened the stopcock.

"You do not want chloroform in your LSD. Chloroform causes violent irritation and inflammation of the mucous membranes. You do not want impurities in your LSD. Impurities cause side effects and disrupt the clarity of the trip. I will let you know when the LSD is ready for ingestion. After we collect the mother liquor, we'll work under the hood to evaporate the chloroform from the liquid base."

As soon as the chromatography was done, he headed for the back room, with the LSD as a base dissolved in chloroform. We followed. I couldn't help noticing that Tim had a flat ass with very little flesh, unlike Owsley's cheery round derriere.

Owsley was shouting above the sound of the machinery. "We must boil off the chloroform at the lowest temperature achievable to keep the LSD away from heat." He explained his new process of flash evaporation, but the vacuum pump was so loud, I could not hear him. I opened the door and split.

"Melissa, Rhoney, come here." Owsley wanted us present for the final step, turning the LSD into ingestible form. I certainly would not miss this! We came running.

In a flask was the dry LSD base. He dissolved it in methanol and converted it into the salt by adding the proportional amount of tartaric acid and evaporating the methanol. He had worked hard calculating reactions to perfect the crystallization process. After his failure to evaporate the methanol with vacuum desiccation, he tried pushing crystallization at a very cold freeze but got a sludge with a lot of impurities in it, and if you ingested that, the high was a bad trip. The LSD had to be pure and the crystal formation right. He cooled the LSD in solution with methanol slowly until crystals formed, then placed the crystalline LSD in a dry, covered flask to prevent moisture contamination.

"Here, Melissa." Owsley handed her a round-bottomed flask with a ground-glass stopper. "Take the tails and racemize the iso-LSD. I think we can convert it to 88% normal by racemization."

"Right! I'll use 50% tartaric acid." We used tartaric acid to form the salt for the LSD because it had four physical isomers, three of which were optically active, the observed rotation useful in calculating concentration. All four isomers were soluble in water, which added to its usefulness. Owsley followed Melissa to the lab bench.

I was jealous.

Upstairs, I rummaged through our collection of tapes and put on a cassette by David Crosby. I moved my body in time to the beat and repeated the refrain: "What can we do now that we both love you."

Owsley came upstairs and waltzed into my arms. He whispered, "Open your mouth." I opened my mouth, and he put a drop of LSD under my tongue.

"Ooh!" I shook my head at the bitter taste.

"La, la, la," went his tongue and he caressed my mouth and licked my face and panted with desire. "Just want to make love to you. Now you're not jealous."

Mile-High Blues

Something unusual was going on in our triangle. It was spring. Melissa was returning to the Bay Area to spend more time with Jack Casady, and Owsley was also going to California, leaving Tim and me to do the work. Before he left, Bear carefully weighed out the starting material and began the synthesis. He would return when we were further along in the process. Owsley had placed the standard order with the butcher the day before he left, so I picked up the order despite the fact that Tim favored peanut butter sandwiches on white bread and I was a small carnivore. Bear wanted to maintain our standard Denver appearances. The refrigerator was full of meat. Soon Tim made a couple of passes at me, but I thought about it and decided I'd rather have him as a friend.

While Bear was in California, he flew to LA to hang out with his friend Mama Cass, who was involved in planning a three-day outdoor music festival at Monterey. Owsley promised to psychedelicize the event. It would be a tall order to synthesize that much LSD and turn it into tabs, but Owsley was determined to provide the best acid for the festival.

In less than a week, he was back in Denver, without Melissa, but with a really cute guy named Johnny Altman, as in Altman's Department Stores from the 1930s to the 1960s. He was part of the "pleasure crew": trust-fund babies who followed the psychedelic scene backstage and beyond. Entry was won with trust money that paid the tab (as with Tim Leary and the Mellon family). Johnny was tall and solid, with shoulder-length hair, casual pants, a banker's shirt, and dockside shoes. Very politely he invited me to take a ride with him to Boulder in the convertible sports car he had rented.

Owsley did not want me to go.

"Please," I begged. "I haven't been out of the lab except to ride my bike to the butcher's."

He was reading about chromatography and with his wire-rimmed glasses and long hair, he looked like

Benjamin Franklin with his balls hanging out. The final stage of the LSD synthesis was crystallization—"running the columns." Owsley was comparing the rates of recovery of product, using the circumference of the column as the variable. A larger diameter column might speed up the process by decreasing the friction along the sides. He was willing to consider any design that would give us a better yield, even if we had to hassle packing both sizes of columns, 40 millimeters and 55 millimeters, even if it meant double the amount of glassware to wash.

I looked over his shoulder at the diagrams and rubbed his neck.

"We'll be back by sunset."

"Go. Get out of here."

I jumped into the sports car, and we headed up the mountain to find Boulder. We ascended rather quickly to 7,000 feet and ended up at a fraternity bar in a college town. We were high on acid and found the scene immature and depressing. We left quickly and wended our way back down the mountain as the sun set over the Rockies. The stars seemed almost close enough to touch, but back at the lab reality set in. What kind of yield would we get? That was on all our minds. Tim and I, true to the Virgo stereotype, were both champion worriers.

This was the second time I had done the process. In the back room the vacuum pumps hummed, and the sweet smell of chloroform seeped through the door. Here in a windowless room in Denver, I was doing important work. As Monterey Pop approached, we worked around the clock to make the LSD.

Monterey Pop and Jimi Hendrix

On June 16, Owsley and I flew from Denver to Monterey. I was dressed in expensive clothes with my hair pinned up and little pearls in my ears. I was trying to look unobtrusive, unlike Owsley who dressed as usual, wearing his many-pocketed leather vest and weather-worn bear claw necklace. He was carrying on his person enough LSD to turn on the entire event, about 100,000 tabs, half the size of aspirin, dyed purple—Monterey Purple—270 micrograms each, as well as his Murine bottle of 99.9% pure liquid LSD of which one healthy drop was enough. In his vest pocket was a dark bottle of thick hashish oil that looked black until you realized it was very dark green and about an ounce of excellent sativa, a strain of cannabis that was hallucinatory. He never thought twice about it.

"You're a Virgo, you worry." He felt completely cool and laughed. "I always look different and I enjoy it."

Long hair was unusual and hippies were subjected to discrimination. But at that time flying was considered first-class travel, and there was no airport security. As we took our seats on the Rocky Mountain airliner, I couldn't help feeling a little jealous again. We were meeting Melissa and the Jefferson Airplane at the Bay Motel. So Melissa had Jack, Melissa had Owsley, and I shared Owsley with Melissa. I didn't like it.

"Wake up!" Owsley rustled me to look out my window. "Check out the weather." We changed seats. "Heavy cloud cover! No way the pilot can land in these conditions," Bear said, mostly to himself.

There was an announcement on the PA: we were going to land in San Jose.

I looked at my watch. It was already six o'clock. Owsley began ranting that if he could not make it to the festival, the music would not have the transformative effect.

"Yes," I said, "forge a union between England and the United States, unite all blues singers—black and white, man and woman. 'Oh, the ink is black, and the page is white, together we—'"

"Shut up, Rhoney, I am thinking. We can still make it before the bands go on. Monterey is an hour's drive from San Jose." He looked at his watch for the eighth time in ten minutes and stopped talking. Was there anything I could say to make him feel better?

"Bear, remember the time I was on a flight to Europe, high on LSD, and the plane had engine trouble and returned to San Francisco?"

"What's your point, Rhoney? That was a mechanical problem; this is weather."

There was no point. Bear was too logical.

We were the first people off the plane, the first to get our luggage, and the first in line to get on the bus to Monterey, both of us laden with gear.

"Strong like Bear," he joked. He was happy again.

"Fifty more miles," I responded, happy too as the door finally opened.

The driver waved at us from his seat at the top of the steps.

"No, no. You cannot take all this on the bus. You must put it underneath."

Bear growled but did what he was told.

We were on the bus, separated from our gear and late for the Monterey Pop Festival. Bouncing up and down in the back of the bus, Bear looked at a typed page of the lineup of musicians and pointed out whose performance we had already missed.

"You don't even like Simon and Garfunkel." I started singing "Scarborough Fair," then looked at his face. "You hate that song. You think it's meaningless."

"That's not the point." Again, there was no point.

"Who else is on tonight?" I asked.

"Eric Burdon."

"Oh, The Animals."

I sang, "'There is a house in New Orleans. They call . . .'" I looked at Bear. He had put his hands over his ears.

"Please, spare me."

He reached into his vest and surreptitiously dosed himself from the Murine bottle, then as an afterthought offered a dose to me. I refused. I was plenty high already, and I hadn't had a full night's sleep in several days. He was getting more excited while I was falling asleep.

We arrived at the motel where all the bands were staying, and Melissa came out to help, directing us to go immediately to the backstage area to get our passes. I bundled my alpaca poncho around me. Although it was almost summertime, I felt the chill of the breeze off the Pacific and started to shiver. I pinned up my hair with more hairpins and followed Owsley backstage to the sign-in table.

Backstage, Ravi Shankar, the foremost Indian musician in the world, was standing with his accompanist, classical tabla player Alla Rakha, and Owsley's old friend Jean Millay. She was a strong supporter of the medicinal use of LSD. She was sure that LSD could enable reimprinting in traumatic disorders and even prove beneficial in the treatment of schizophrenia.

Owsley was always polite—his Southern gentlemanly manners—and offered Ravi Shankar a dose of LSD from the Murine bottle. Ravi Shankar turned sharply away as if insulted, and without a word, he stormed out of the room. Maybe Ravi Shankar was high on the natch. Certainly that was a possibility. LSD was not for everyone. But his expression was dour and his mood not sweet.

Had Owsley unknowingly breached an Indian custom? I turned to Jean Millay.

"What was that all about?"

She looked at Alla Rakha who was smiling, his hands folded in front of his white Indian dress. She placed her hands, like him, in namaste mudra position and said nothing to me. What was THAT about?

Bear offered me a drop from the Murine bottle, and I accepted, lifting my tongue as he squirted the LSD into my mouth.

The acid kicked in just as Janis Joplin went on. We were in the wings with the rest of the Grateful Dead. Pigpen sometimes joined Janis, but not tonight. Albert Grossman knew the movie *Monterey Pop* was being made by D. A. Pennebaker, and he had plans for Janis that were exclusive. Whatever Janis took that night, it helped her make history. She knocked everyone out.

By the end of the evening, my ears were ringing. Walking back to the motel, the ocean air wetted my face. I fell into bed, but not Owsley. Later I heard he was up all night giving away LSD.

Ravi Shankar opened on Sunday afternoon. I took more acid; the whole audience was high on acid. We made sure everyone but the Indian musicians got a hit of LSD.

Ravi explained that he would play an alat solo before
the tabla joined in, and that he had selected an afternoon
raga because the sun was late to set over the Pacific, and it
was not the correct time for an evening raga. I was glad. I
wanted the audience to love Indian music, and I felt that for
the initiate the lightness of an afternoon raga was preferable
to the darkness of the evening raga, even if it were played in
fast tintal—sixteen beats. I sat in the audience in the sunshine
and listened. I was feeling no grudge against Ravi Shankar
for his disdain of LSD, especially as we had gotten excellent
seats near the sound booth. The sound booth was always the
best spot to hear the music. Jean Millay moved her hands in
a ritual dance, counting out the rhythm, and I copied her.
Soon others in the audience were imitating her gestures—
clap, clap, open, clap, come in on the one. It was as if we
were in a trance, powerless to resist, powerful in the shared
motion, and the connection to the harmonies of the sitar and
the rhythmic beat of the drum, counting out the measures in
double and triple time.

I went backstage during the Blues Project. The guitar
player, Danny, had been my first lover. I stood on the side
of the stage, whistling and cheering when they came off.

"How'd I do? How'd ya like my guitar? How'd my
voice sound?" Danny asked and kissed me.

"The audience was dancing!" I said. Every performer
craves confirmation from the audience. Musicians love to
hear the audience was dancing.

The Who were truly amazing, but when Townsend
smashed his guitar, the violence turned me off. Who did
The Who think they were? Here I was at a festival of love
and peace, watching first-rate musicians smash and burn
their guitars. Did inspiration and destruction dance side
by side? What did I know?

Owsley went around chanting, "Hoo, hoo." He resembled an owl with his big round glasses and the flapping of his arms.

I saw Jimi Hendrix backstage, and he looked wild. His eyes darted in and out without focus, and he had a slithering quality to his movements as if he were everywhere at once, as if he he were possessed by a dybbuk, like the people at my black nanny's church who spoke in tongues and danced and writhed. My father often accused me of having a dybbuk inside.

Owsley fawned over Jimi. From what magical realm did that music emerge? To Owsley, it spake from an inner depth that was surely psychedelic.

The Lips of Wisdom Are Closed Except to the Ears of Understanding*

When Jimi Hendrix appeared at the Fillmore West in San Francisco, June 20 through June 24, 1967, the backstage was full of black people. This was unusual in the psychedelic rock scene. Many of the musicians and almost all of the fans were white. But Jimi, despite the fact that he was part Native American, considered himself black, and had invited his whole family from Seattle and all his relatives in Oakland to come to the show. The backstage area was so crowded with Jimi's relatives that management was holding back the regulars, but Owsley was insistent that he speak to Jimi.

We walked up to the stage door to the venue.

"I'm Bear," he announced to a burly roadie with a clipboard with a list. "The Experience knows I'm here."

"Okay, man. You can go in. Who's she?" Security pointed to me.

*The Kybalion

"She's with me."

Jimi was surrounded by his family. A big, old black woman wearing a big straw hat with flowers was hugging him while he laughed. The way she held Jimi reminded me of the only hugs I got as a child—big bosom hugs from black women hired by my mother.

Jimi wore colorful scarfs, a silk shirt, a silver necklace and bracelet with turquoise stones. Bear began his rap, explaining that the music he heard in his head was the music that Jimi played. He wanted to record Jimi live, not the band, just Jimi high on LSD playing the guitar.

"That music will be something else." Bear gestured with his hand like a symphony conductor.

They shared a hearty laugh and lit up Owsley's DMT pipe. The smoke from the crystals on mint leaves gave off an acrid odor.

"Jack Casady coming?" Jimi asked, taking a puff. He loved Jack's bass playing.

Bear nodded while holding the smoke in his lungs. That would be easy. Jack always said yes to Bear. Suddenly, the show was over, and somehow Bear arranged for two cars to take us to the Masonic Temple at the top of Nob Hill on California and Taylor Streets.

Jimi stood on the cold granite steps, his guitar flung over his back, his thin, winsome body dressed in colors. A frieze on the temple represented the struggle between the forces of good and evil, but the presentation was somber. The Masons were a secret society. They discriminated against Jews; they excluded women from membership. What were we doing here?

It was that quiet time of night when nothing stirred. A shiver went up my spine.

Bear carried in his Norelco compact cassette recorder

and a Fender amp for Jimi. We followed him to a dark
room with heavy draperies covering the windows. Above
the mantle over the fireplace were ritualistic paintings
that looked more like emblems than art. I watched Jimi
dart around the room, his silk pants shimmering purple.
Melissa and I shared an overstuffed chair.

Owsley lit a fire and the room brightened up. He set up
a stage area to the right of the fireplace, then took out the
LSD. We all smiled and chatted as Owsley administered the
drops from the Murine bottle. I rolled a joint from Bear's
stash as he set up the recording equipment, and Melissa put
another log on the fire.

Jimi sat in a chair with his guitar, plugged in the amp,
and started to play. Owsley scuttled around him, moving the
microphone, listening to Jimi with earphones and adjusting
the controls. Jack left. Bear was recording Jimi solo.

Melissa and I unfurled our legs so our toes touched.
I closed my eyes. In and out of the music I moved,
searching for order, for harmony, but all I could feel was
chaos. The walls of the place curved in like a tomb. Jimi's
mass of hair hid him as he sat in a chair, hunched over his
guitar, turned away from us; his fingers moved as if they
were on fire. He played discordant chords, disembodied
sounds I never associated with guitar.

When Jimi stopped playing, he stood up and stretched
like a cat. Melissa had fallen asleep on the couch and Jack
was still not back. Bear held up the cassette triumphantly.
I pulled aside the heavy drapes to see if the sun had risen,
and the light blinded me. I groped for my shades.

"Hey, man, let me see that tape." Jimi took the tape
out of Bear's hand, walked over to the fireplace and
threw it into the fire. An acidic smell filled the room as
the flames hit the acetate. Jimi smiled, grabbed his guitar,

and spirited out the door. I stared at the fire, mesmerized, watching the blue-white flames. Bear tried to get the tape out of the fire, but it was gone.

Jack entered trying to fan away the smoke with his hands, "What happened?"

Owsley couldn't find words. Jack grinned, his luscious lips almost inverting, and started talking about breakfast with Melissa.

Bear said, "Fuck."

Self-Transforming Machine Elves

Nick, my Sir Lancelot from Brooklyn, visited us in
Berkeley. We sat at the kitchen table smoking weed
while Owsley talked about the work we would do when
we returned to the Denver lab. With Nick, a fellow
underground chemist, he was frank.

Nick asked, "Have you synthesized any DMT?"

Nick took a package out of his traveling bag and
showed us a brown-tinged glob of crystal. Bear stuck his
clawlike pinky into it and put a taste into his mouth.

He grimaced, shaking his head repeatedly. I bent down
to smell it and made a face.

"Idiots," Nick exclaimed. "It's impure. Would you like
to try your hand at purifying it?"

"Why don't you let Rhoney have a go at it?" Bear
suggested. "She's taking organic chemistry at UC Berkeley."

I was attending both the lecture and the lab. I already
knew a lot about the glassware setups and the procedures,
but now I was learning concepts. Time to drop out. Bear
and I were returning to Denver.

"Sure," I said and listened carefully.

"DMT crystallizes out at two melting points. The
higher melting point crystals are larger and harder to grow
because you have to keep the liquid from crystallizing
out at the lower melting point, but it's worth the effort.
DMT crystals are the most beautiful crystals, white and
hexagonal, like snowflakes."

Nick taught me that DMT crystals were formed from

solution when the solution was evaporated or cooled below the saturation point. Dependent on the skill of the operator, the crystals could melt at 54 degrees centigrade or 72 degrees centigrade. The higher melting point crystals were the purer form.

"But Nick, how do I do it?"

"Slowly! Avoid supersaturation."

I thought, yeah, that would cause immediate seed crystal formation. In such a short time as a student I had learned so much.

As we hugged goodbye, Nick added, "Now don't forget to take a sample and test the melting point. Don't worry about wasting it. I have plenty more."

I had a specific hallucination under DMT: the ground rotated 15 degrees and everything was at a slant. Was this a manifestation of the earth's rotational axis? Was there a shift happening and now I saw it? The ground was not down, nothing was at right angles, up was sideways, and when I jumped up and down, thinking I could right the deviation, nothing happened. I had no control. Reality did not return. My world remained at a tilt. Luckily the effects of DMT were short acting.

When we returned to the Denver lab I set up a closet to purify the DMT and worked late at night, when everyone was sleeping. I dissolved the DMT slurry in a round-bottomed flask with the correct amount of the solvent, n-hexane, in a ratio of 100 to 1. I used a whirring rod and a hot plate and did not overheat the DMT. Once a uniform solution formed, I added a seed crystal from the original supply and slowly cooled it to evaporate the solvent and initiate crystallization. I watched the solution to see if any crystals were forming too rapidly and stirred to break up the crystals before that point. As the solution began to solidify, I placed the flask in the refrigerator. Facets of crystals emerged like diamonds. At the end of the procedure, I melted a sample. The thermometer read 72 degrees centigrade. Nick's directions were perfect. I had succeeded in growing pure DMT crystals. I ran upstairs to tell Tim and Bear.

Tim was sitting on the couch, his legs crossed, reading a fat science fiction paperback. Bear was nude at the kitchen table reading a technical text.

The phone rang. I stopped and stared at it. Phone calls were unusual in our secret location. Few had our number. Owsley kept a book full of valued phone numbers, meticulously guarding the numbers of well-known musicians, actors, dealers, connected people of class, heirs and heiresses, but seldom did he share our phone number. Some might say he was secretive, but we thought of him as protective.

Bear answered. "What's up? What is it?" He unfolded his knees and changed position. His bare ballet dancer legs were shapely and muscular, and he had big balls. He spoke in a crisp, no-nonsense voice, and you could hear the air passing through his nostrils and into his respiratory tract, as if he were executing a singing or acting lesson. Acting was another discipline he had studied, but like me, he was without a great sense of humor. He bent over the phone, listening intently. There was a long period of silence. This was also unusual.

Finally, he hung up and said, "It's Melissa. She's coming back to the lab."

The night Melissa arrived, the tension was high. She smiled but did not say much. Soon she went into the master bedroom and closed the door. Owsley followed.

I needed comfort from Tim. We took the other bedroom. I threw off my clothes with abandon and lay naked on the bed, watching Tim neatly fold his plaid shirt, his cords with the belt still on, finally removing his white Hanes underwear. I stared. He was big and skinny and curved. He placed his clothes in a pile on the floor next to the bed. Carefully, he removed his eyeglasses and climbed on top of me, just like that. He was a big guy and I could barely move, but he was quiet and gentle.

The next day, we all gathered as Bear weighed the LSD crystal on an analytic balance and wrapped it for travel. We had finished the synthesis and were ready to leave. At another place we would turn the LSD into tablets. Tim would continue at the Denver lab. First he was planning to run the sludge through the chromatography columns to get more pure LSD. He wanted me to stay.

"I can run the tails through the columns again and again for more product. Purification and recovery are just as important as the synthesis," he declared generously. I agreed, but I was ready to leave Denver.

"Help me with STP synthesis," Tim enticed me. We had used an easy synthesis process that produced a high yield on a very small sample, and STP was still legal. The Feds had not yet figured out its molecular structure.

Bear piped up, "Rhoney, get ready to leave the lab. We're going home!" That was enough for me. Tim topped Bear's salary and I still said no. No amount of money Tim offered could dissuade me from going with Bear. He thought we were a family. Even Melissa couldn't take that away.

When it came to packing, Owsley discarded nothing. He was the ultimate, consummate packer, neatly wrapping packages and arranging them in the trunks. Whatever was contraband was well hidden. Owsley was the expert, and Melissa and I followed his direction. Bear decided today was the day we were leaving Denver. No more tea with water that never boiled.

Tim bent down to kiss me goodbye.

We arrived at the airport, and while Owsley bought our tickets, Melissa and I sat on the trunks and attempted to look ordinary. Even when we dressed down, we stood out in our short skirts and tie-dyes, our long Rapunzel-like hair. We had a saying: "LSD makes the hair grow long."

Melissa looked me in the eye and spoke quietly, "I told Owsley that I've moved in with Jack."

"What?" I exclaimed.

She chuckled at my speechlessness.

Owsley appeared across the ticketing area, pushing a cart and waving the plane tickets in his hand. He assumed he was inconspicuous, but we could smell his patchouli from across the room.

A Decent Proposal

We arrived at SFO from Denver in less than four hours and found Owsley's car in the airport parking lot.

He said, "Let's go to Berkeley first."

"If we're dropping Melissa at Jack's, it's closer to the airport than Berkeley." I knew what would happen. Melissa would get to Owsley's house and stay. I would never be alone with Owsley.

"Not if we take the San Mateo bridge," Owsley said matter-of-factly.

When we arrived, Bob Thomas greeted us and we sat around the kitchen table smoking a joint. Melissa showed no signs of leaving. Owsley was up all night unpacking. I crashed on the couch, and in the morning when I awoke I heard Melissa chatting away in the kitchen.

Owsley said, "We're going up to campus to see Alan. He has agreed to run specs on the LSD."

Alan was getting his PhD in organic chemistry and had a fully equipped lab with an infrared absorption spectrometer. Owsley intended to run spectroscopy on the LSD we had made in Denver to test its purity.

The three of us headed up to Latimer Hall, the new chemistry building on the UC Berkeley campus, and took the stairs to Alan's lab. The test would have to wait. Alan was too busy with his research. Melissa had just gotten off the phone. Jack was back and she had to go to San Francisco. Bear agreed to take her.

Alan said, "Why don't you stay? I'll show you the spectrometer." Maybe he felt an affinity because we were both Jewish. Maybe he felt bad for me because I was part of a love triangle.

They left and I stayed. They were together and I was alone. Alan was sitting at his lab bench, preoccupied with calculations. "Where's the bathroom?" I asked

Alan explained in this male-dominated science building, bathrooms for the ladies were on every other floor and unfortunately his floor had only men's rooms. It was late at night, and no one else was in the building. I wandered out of the lab, down empty corridors, into a stairwell, down to another floor, as if I were in an Escher painting. Bear's rejection of me was devastating, and I raced along the hallways wild with jealousy. When Alan asked me to stay with him, I said yes. The following day I woke up in Alan's king-size bed. Owsley phoned. He wanted me to come home. "Melissa's in San Francisco with Jack," he told me.

I repeated, "Melissa!"

"Are you attracted to Melissa?" I asked Alan.

He shook his head.

"I never notice Melissa. She's not my type." He had a Chicago accent.

"Don't you think Melissa and I look alike? We're both the same size; we have the same color hair; we both have blue eyes."

"You and Melissa are nothing alike. You are verbal; she is quiet. Melissa dropped out of school. You are Jewish and educated. I would marry you. I wouldn't marry Melissa."

Alan wrapped blankets around me and brought me a tray with a banana and peanut butter sandwich on white bread, as if he were a Jewish mother.

"What!" I exclaimed. "This is not Jewish food. Jews don't eat white bread."

Though I could joke, I was too upset to eat. Alan heated up a tray of Chinese food for me. The smell was enticing, but I wasn't hungry. He sat on the corner of the bed. "Marry me," he said.

If Bear weren't the sound man for the Grateful Dead, I would have considered Alan's proposal, but the Grateful Dead magic was still more appealing.

Then there was sex with Owsley, of course. When I got back to the Berkeley house, Owsley was alone, reading in the kitchen nude. I unbuckled my cowboy belt. My jeans fell to the floor in a vortex. I leaned my body against his and lined myself up so our genitalia touched. Who was hornier? We laughed.

"By the way," he said, "Alan told me our LSD tested 99.9% pure."

A Gift from Hell's Angels

The doorbell rang. Owsley was on the phone, and we were still undressed although it was late morning.

"Get the door, Rhoney," Bear called.

I unlatched the lock and greeted a big Hell's Angel with a bushy beard and a bird cage. I noticed the swastika on his helmet. My mother was a Zionist and a former local president of Hadassah in Westchester County, but I was not my mother.

"Hi. I'm Terry the Tramp." He smiled. He looked familiar. He was the Angel I had met at the Med on Telegraph Avenue in Berkeley.

He opened the cage and moved his big hand toward a bird with brown feathers and piercing gold eyes. "An owl for Owsley," he proclaimed as the bird perched on his hand. Owsley put out his hand and immediately the owl moved to his finger.

"Wow!" I exclaimed. "What a gift! Where'd ya get it?"

The doorbell rang again. This time it was Melissa. "Hoohah," she called.

Boohoo, I thought.

"Come in, Melissa. Guess what? Terry the Tramp brought us an owl."

"Screech, screech," she laughed.

Owsley said, "Perfect name, Melissa. We'll call him Screech."

He went to the bookshelf and took down *Field Guide to Owls of North America*, sat at the table scanning the pages, and asked for tea. Melissa brewed his favorite brand of Farmers Brothers' tea. He had researched their growing methods and determined they were the best source for local black pekoe.

Owsley cupped his hand over the owl's small round head. "This way, he won't fly away."

Melissa asked, "Can I hold him?"

She put out her hand and the owl hopped onto her finger. She lifted the owl to her head and it nestled into her thick hair. She picked up the teapot, walked gracefully around the table, pouring more tea, while the owl stayed on her head.

Terry the Tramp passed around a joint. The owl flew from Melissa's head and landed on a ceiling beam.

Owsley looked up from reading and said, "I think Screech is a burrowing owl. He will need to be fed a live mouse once a week to keep his digestion functioning properly, and the rest of the time, he can eat insects, like crickets or grasshoppers. Burrowing owls, unlike other owls, also eat fruits and seeds, but we'll keep him on a low-carb diet."

I wondered who would feed the owl. Would I be the one?

Owsley settled it. He chose Melissa.

"Melissa, why don't you take your car and get a live mouse now? There's a pet shop on San Pablo. Get a healthy mouse for Screech. He looks underfed!" He gave Terry the Tramp a look of disapproval, as if the Hell's Angels had purposely starved the owl.

"Why do you think the owl is a male?" I asked provocatively. "It has such a small head and plain feathers. Aren't the males brightly feathered?"

"You are incorrect. Unlike most owls, where the female is actually larger than the male, with burrowing owls the sexes are the same size." I leaned over Owsley to look at his book. He was sitting in a chair pulled under the table with crossed legs, completely nude. I looked at his lap. He pointed to the book. I moved my eyes.

"Oh, it says here that the male of the species is vocal. He makes a coo-coo or a hoo-hoo sound. Have you heard it, Terry?" I asked.

"No," he replied.

"Well then, maybe the owl's not a male! The females are quiet!" I declared.

Tramp spoke softly, "I've never heard the owl make any noises." He looked like a big, tough Santa Claus, with tattoos around his bulky arms and metal bracelets with spikes around his wrists. He was one of Owsley's few chosen distributors. Our new LSD had yet to be tabulated.

Owsley said, "Rhoney, as part of my crew, you must have a California driver's license. You failed your California driving test."

"Only once, Bear."

"Fine. This time Terry will take you for the road test in Richmond, where our old lab was. It's a warehouse district—fewer cars, people. If Terry is responsible for you, you'll pass."

"Bear, get real, Terry rides a bike, not a car," I said.

"We'll take the club car for your test, but I can show you my motorcycle now, give you a demo," Terry offered.

"Don't pass this up," Bear advised.

Terry handed me a spare helmet, and I climbed on the back of his Harley Chopper and put my arms around his waist, watched his feet in his heavy boots take the pedals. "If you're a member of the Richmond chapter, why does your vest say Oakland?"

He was wearing his club vest, embroidered on the back with a winged skull.

"I'm a member of both chapters," he confided, "an officer in Oakland."

We roared up the dead-end street in front of our house.

The day of the test arrived and Terry came over to Valley Street early, driving an ordinary American car, but wearing a Hell's Angels jacket that read "HELL'S ANGELS, RICHMOND."

We drove to Richmond, I at the wheel with my learner's permit and he in the passenger seat. First I took the written test, answering questions in a booklet sitting on a bench, Terry the Tramp beside me. I finished quickly and was graded a perfect score. Terry acted very impressed with my performance, but I told him, "The written test is easy. It's the driving test that's hard. I hate to park."

"Have you ever played pool?" he asked me.

"Yeah, we had a pool table in our house growing up."

"Parking is like playing pool. Think of the angle. Take the car back as if you are a cue ball striking the side of the table. Aim for the exact spot to head the ball toward the pocket."

The examiner did not stop Terry the Tramp when he climbed into the backseat. When it came time to parallel park, he signaled me when to cut the turn. I parked perfectly. Even the rigid official smiled when he told me I passed. Terry the Tramp did not say a word during the entire test, but after the test, when we were driving off, he at the wheel, he said, "Let me show you the Hell's Angels' headquarters."

We went to a large detached two-story house in a quasi-suburban neighborhood of the East Bay with stately houses and small lawns. Terry explained this was just a getaway house and only the officers had the key. Inside, the windows were covered with heavy drapes and the interior was furnished with carpets and comfortable couches. I asked about the swastika.

"I'm Jewish," I told Terry. He explained the swastika was an ancient symbol of friendship, and he respected the beauty and intelligence of Jewish women.

"Do you agree with Owsley that the best way to know someone is to make love with them?" I asked.

If I Had Not Let Go

Sex with Owsley was the best. He was completely uninhibited, and his goal was to please me. He was always ready for more loving and had no inhibitions about making love on the spot. I never wore protection. What if I got pregnant? I thought about having a child. Back and forth I went, considering the choices. I heard my mother's shrill voice saying, "You'll never have your own man." But the old patterns were no longer valid. We had experienced expanded consciousness and could create a new kind of family. I wondered what kind of father Owsley would be. He already had two children years before he took LSD, and he never saw them.

I gave my father one of my infrequent phone calls, and he asked for my address. I told him I'd call him back.

"Bear," I asked, "what address should I give my father?"

"I don't want any mail coming here." He thought for a minute. "You can give him the post office box in Berkeley. I'll add your name."

"I bet my father's sending me a check. That's his way of showing affection."

"No worries. You're with me," Bear said and gave me a kiss.

Our post office was in downtown Berkeley. We went there every other day. It wasn't unusual for us to be followed by law enforcement. Sure enough, an unmarked sedan was following our rented VW Bug. Bear was annoyed and headed for the Berkeley Hills, downshifting as we climbed. He made hairpin turns at top speed, turned around at one curve and headed down, hoping to lose the tail, but the agent was good. He turned in aggressive pursuit. I felt nauseous.

"What if I were pregnant, Bear? I'd lose the baby."

"You're pregnant?"

"I wish. Bear, I'm carsick. I don't want a lecture. I just want to get a letter. If you told me the combination, I could have gone on my own. You gave it to Melissa."

Owsley spoke in a very rational voice. "Melissa is the way it has to be right now. I don't need for you to be freaking out."

He ground the gears and the car nearly clipped a corner. I held on to my seat and the door handle.

"Stay cool. I'm gonna lose that fucker, and then you can get your damn letter." Bear focused on the car and the road. We reached the top of Grizzly Peak where Bear stomped on the accelerator and smoked the car. Tires screaming, he spun the VW 180 degrees so we were going the other way as the agent came flying over the hill and off into the Oakland Hills. I was thrilled in spite of myself.

The post office was closed, but the lobby with its hundreds of post office boxes in the walls was open. I couldn't believe that Bear would not give me the combination. It was so unfair. Melissa knew it, too.

"Everyone knows I'm connected to you so you're not even protecting me. My name is on the box," I said, clenching my jaw.

Bear bent over and turned the combination so I couldn't see. He stood up. He fanned out a whole bunch of mail, and I quickly spotted my father's rambling handwriting. I attempted to pull the letter out of his grubby hands, but he pushed me away. I was surprised by his aggression and almost fell on the floor. He finally handed me the letter, and I ripped open the envelope, but no check fell out. It was another one of my father's typical letters assuming I was wrong.

I snapped. "You're so mean to me. You don't value me." I wanted to slap his face.

"You are hysterical. I'm leaving."

I rushed after him, desperate, out of my mind. He started the car. I grabbed the handle. If I had not let go, I would have been dragged along the street. I let go.

Buddy Miles Interlude

We had bonded with Buddy Miles at Monterey Pop, where he drummed with Michael Bloomfield, Paul Butterfield, and The Electric Flag. Buddy was a strong drummer, a sought-after studio side man—a big, powerful black guy. He would soon be with Jimi Hendrix in Band of Gypsies.

When Buddy arrived at our home in Berkeley, Bear brought out a big doobie of sinsemilla and lit up. Soon we were all laughing and talking. Buddy and I were both Virgos and we mused on that. "My real name is George," he whispered in my ear, leaning over his Sumo-sized girth.

Bear put a hefty amount of hashish oil in a glass pipe he had designed specifically for this purpose. He lit the pipe and passed it to Buddy, who took a long drag. Then he held the pipe out to me.

I took a toke. It was smooth, almost like opium.

Suddenly, Buddy clutched his heart. "I'm having a heart attack," he croaked. "I'm dying. Help, help me. I can't breathe. Heart attacks run in my family. And lung collapse. I'm gonna die. My heart's racing a mile a minute. Please, save me. Take me to the hospital."

Bear looked aghast. He hated hospitals and doctors. We walked out—Buddy between us—Owsley helping support his big bulk as we put him in the passenger seat. I jumped into the driver's seat and drove quickly to Herrick Hospital in Berkeley. I ran into the ER to get help and came back with an orderly and a wheelchair. We wheeled Buddy into the hospital and into a private cubicle. Buddy was fast deteriorating and gasping for breath, slumped in the wheelchair.

"Quick," said the nurse, "let's get him onto a gurney and hook him up to a cardiac monitor."

We lifted part of his body onto the metal gurney, but it slipped down and his leg hit the floor with a thud. I giggled and even Buddy started to laugh. What a sight—this mass of flesh, half on a gurney. The nurse had undone Buddy's shirt to clear his airways in case his breathing got worse, and his chest was hanging out. The famous drummer was as vulnerable as a child. Buddy looked at me conspiratorially and rolled his eyes. We had agreed not to mention what Buddy had ingested prior to the attack. The EKG was started and as soon as the rhythm printed, the doctor asked to speak to me privately, showing me that the cardiogram demonstrated that the patient had a normal rhythm. Buddy was only having an anxiety attack. When we told Buddy the good news, he took a big breath, moved his hands as if he were playing a drum riff, and said, "Thank you world, but I bet you one day, I'll die this way."

I sighed with relief, grateful that the hashish had not caused Buddy Miles to have a heart attack and die, that he had simply gotten too stoned and went paranoid. Good pot.

Day of the Wolf, Night of the Beatle

In Berkeley in the summer of 1967, the Ali Akbar Khan School of Indian Music opened to teach Westerners the fundamentals of Indian rhythm and melody. The school offered classes in sarod, sitar, and tabla, but not Indian dance, despite the fact that Sam Scripps had endowed the school because his wife fell in love with Indian dance.

In India, music is venerated, and musicians have a family tradition of performance that can be traced back generations. Ustad Ali Akbar Khan, a master of sarod, headed the Berkeley school. He was from Northern India, of high caste, and a Muslim; in Arabic *ustad* means "master." Unlike Hindus, he was not a vegetarian, but unlike most Muslims, he loved his scotch.

Some of my East Coast friends who were devotees of Indian music attended, and so did I. On the first day, I arrived at the school late. Everything else was secondary to making LSD, and my friends at Indian music school knew what I was doing but not where. I had promised Owsley I would not talk about our project. Classes were over for the day; it was mealtime, but the serious students spent as much time as possible with the teachers and took meals with them. They were in the kitchen where a curry dish was cooking. Julie, my childhood friend from Camp Willowway, was there talking to the master. Her long frame was draped in a chair at the table, her slender fingers gesturing in dialogue. She was a standup comedienne, a cabaret singer, a folk-song balladeer, an actress, and now a student of

Indian music, studying tabla. Engrossed in conversation with the master, she did not notice me until I was directly in front of her. I bent down and kissed her.

"Dahling," she cooed at me in her seductress voice, "wonderful that you are here. Khansahib, meet my dear friend, Rhoney. You two will love each other. *Khansahib* is a term of endearment, Rhoney. Don't you just love it? I cannot say *Ustad* Ali Akbar Khan whenever I talk to my teacher, right Khansahib?"

She stood up and pulled me in front of Khansahib. Together we bowed. He was a bit overweight, sipping a cocktail, and did not get out of his chair.

"Yes, yes, you are welcome." He nodded his head in greeting.

"We've been talking about the interplay of rhythm and melody. I am considering studying the sarod," Julie said.

"I thought you were here to take tabla," I replied.

"Both, Rhoney. Already I can recite Bilambat Tintal." She chanted:

"*Dha tere kete Dhin-ge Dha tete / Dha-ge Dhin-kata Dhin-ge Dha-tete.*"

She clipped her consonants and rolled her *r*'s and recited the talas.

"What I recited is the rhythm. The *gat* is the composition. I must learn the *gat*, and that usually means a melodic instrument. Of course, it could be rhythm."

Perry, my ex, was sitting on the floor, intently practicing scales on the sitar, counting as he strummed, his bare foot bobbing up and down in rhythm, 1-2-3, 1-2-3, 123-123, 1. He was practicing in the rhythm of a fast tala. Agnes, his girlfriend, complained that she had had polio as a child and sitting in lotus position on the floor for three hours with a heavy sarod was very difficult.

Julie agreed. "You Indians are much smaller. Twisting into a pretzel is no fun."

Shankar, the tabla teacher, was taller. His lips formed a Cupid's bow and his hair was greased like an Indian Elvis Presley. He was wild and sexy, whereas Ali Akbar Khan was meditative and wise.

The delicious aroma of Indian spices filled the air. Shankar cut up vegetables and added spices: saffron, cumin, turmeric, pieces of yellow tamarind rind, ginger, and he tossed them in a saucepan, flipping what looked like spinach into the air, instructing his students to watch his nimble fingers and his limber wrist motion because we would use the same motion when playing tabla. Chanting a count, he danced, and his white silk garment opened to reveal his chocolate thighs.

As I moved my body in time to his rhythm, I realized I could learn Indian dance by studying tabla. "Can I come to Indian music school?" I asked, looking into Khansahib's round, restful face. "I would love to study tabla."

Julie burst out, "Dahling, that is wonderful! You can have my notes."

Shankar said, "I will tutor you," in lilting singsong English.

Every morning before classes we listened to a raga performed by our teachers, sometimes joined by students. Part of the instruction was training our ears to listen. In drum class, we learned to recite the rhythms before we would drum them. Tintal was basic, 16 counts, but there was also 7, 9, 11, 14. I copied the notations from Julie's notebook, but it was extremely complex. Julie had no time to explain. She was on scholarship, and her performance counted. Every spare minute, she practiced.

I invited Shankar to our house in Berkeley to review the rudiments of Indian drumming in a private session. I did

not see Bear's red 1949 Studebaker truck in the driveway.
Shankar carried his drums up the cobblestone path to the
house. I opened the door with my key and walked into the
arched entry hall. Screech the Owl swooped down from
her perch on the high wooden beams and landed on my
head, but when Screech saw that Owsley was not with
me, she flew back up to the beam and hid her head in her
feathers. No one was in the house, and I did not hear any
sounds from Bob's cottage in the back.

Shankar opened the drum case and looked around.
Wide-eyed, he admired our charming brick fairytale house
with its imposing stone hearth and fireplace benches.

I lit a fire in the fireplace. Despite the season, the house
was cool. The windows were stained glass and little sunlight
came through. The fire blazed and the glass eyes of the owl
andirons glowed.

Shankar sat on the floor with his tabla drums, playing
a fast tala in tintal, counting, "1234, 1234, 1234, 1234.
Listen to me. Say the words after me. *Dah din din dah,
dah din din dah, dah tin tin dah, dah tin tin dah.*" He nodded
his head and swayed to the beat, his sharp eyes darting
around me.

"Dah din din din." I stumbled with the words.

"Dance for me," he said with his Indian accent as he
drummed faster and faster, double time, triple time, but
always ending on the 1 in a phrase of 16. "Good. You can
dance even if you can't chant."

I kicked off my leather sandals and danced on the rug,
going closer to him.

Sweating, Shankar stopped drumming, took off his
shirt, hit the drums again, shouted a word to some drum
god. I bent over and touched his chest. His skin was
smooth, hairless.

"Move, dance faster," Shankar shouted.

I twirled around, counting the spins as the number mounted—1-2-3-4, 5-6-7-8, 9-10-11-12, 13-14-15-16, and 1. I opened my arms, palms up as I'd seen the Indians do, and my shirt fell off my shoulder, revealing my breasts. We could not resist, and I pressed myself to his soft chest.

I did not hear Owsley enter the room with his entourage. Shankar stiffened and covered himself. I turned to see Owsley take in the scene.

"You are preoccupied. I see no further reason to be here." He strode away from the living room and stormed out the front door. His voice echoed in my head.

Bear felt the sting of my indiscretion with Shankar and assumed that his lovemaking must be inadequate. His inspiration came in a flash: we needed to make love on wolf skins! He finally found a dealer of exotic pelts in Los Angeles who could come up with a dozen expensive wolf pelts. We were both excited; it was working already. We measured our bed, crawling around as we designed the display of the skins in a circle. Bear said we should leave immediately for LA. The Jefferson Airplane was there, recording their next album and living in a mansion in the Hollywood Hills with a giant pool and many bedrooms. We could shop for wolf skins and stay with the Airplane.

The phone rang. Bear's friend, David Crosby, invited us to LA. George Harrison was in town to see Ravi Shankar at the Hollywood Bowl and wanted to meet Bear.

"Oh, God," I exclaimed, grabbing Bear in the heat of my excitement, "my favorite Beatle!"

"Ooh, la, la, we can get zee wolf skins." He flicked his tongue.

We flew into Burbank and rented a convertible. George Harrison was staying with friends of Ravi Shankar in Hollywood, and we were meeting him later that evening. First we drove to David's in Beverly Glen Canyon, Bear at the wheel.

"What about George?" I attempted a Beatle accent.

Bear moaned. "That's the worst Beatle accent I've ever heard. It sounded Chinese."

The canyon was steep and David lived on the down side of the hill. Luckily, the driveway had a space for our rented car. We climbed the stone stairs to a rustic cottage, and David greeted Bear with an enthusiastic hug around the neck. Joni Mitchell got up from the couch and David introduced us. David and Bear didn't stop talking for a minute. I heard the words but didn't listen to the meaning.

David said, "Why don't you girls go to the local market for some grub?" Bear gave us money.

As soon as we settled in the car, we both lit up cigarettes. "Ugh," I moaned. "Release! Bear won't let me smoke in front of him." Joni was a nonstop smoker and couldn't believe how I bowed to Bear's wishes. Owsley had a vendetta against tobacco. This was more weighty, given his family was from Kentucky. To help me break the tobacco habit, he bought smoking herbs: the herbaceous perennial deer's tongue, so named because its leaves are shaped like a deer's tongue, used to enhance tobacco with the flavor of vanilla; and coltsfoot, an expectorant that causes spasmodic coughing, thus we only added small amounts of it to the smoking mixture. Bear assembled the herbs in stacks, varying the amount of lobelia, the addictive alkaloid in nicotine. I rolled my own cigarettes choosing how much lobelia I needed, depending on whether I wanted more or less of a nicotine hit. This was so much work, and I

coughed so much from the expectorant, I smoked less. Even
this mixture Bear would not allow in the house.

When we got to the store, Joni bought cigarettes and beer,
and I bought cold cuts and farmer's cheese for Bear. Her
brand was Tarryton; mine was Marlboro, but I didn't dare
buy a pack. She bought three cartons.

Back at the house, Joni and I sat on the floor. Bear
offered me some liquid LSD. I couldn't say no.

We raced off to the fur dealer's Beverly Hills mansion.
I stayed in the car and watched the sun set. I was pissed.
We were really late. Bear came out of the darkness
carrying heavy bundles wrapped in string and brown
paper under both arms, tore off a piece of the wrapper,
and nuzzled a fluffy wolf tail under my chin. "Ever feel
that before?"

"No, and I've never met George Harrison before,
either," I moaned.

We got lost in the Hollywood Hills, driving up and
down one long curved road, looking for a house number
in the dark. The top was down and the stars were out, but
the street addresses were hidden. Finally Bear stopped
the car and walked up the street looking for the number.
"Hoohah," he called, "I found it." I jumped out of the car
and ran down the driveway after him.

George apologized for not inviting us inside,
whispering in his Beatle accent that his hosts were asleep.
He looked like a sadhu in a loose Indian Nehru jacket and
baggy pants, but his hair was cut in a page boy, and he
had a walrus mustache. He was very polite and seemed
genuinely thrilled to meet Owsley. He thanked him for the
previous gifts of LSD he had messengered. Owsley took
a baggie of his best out of his leather vest, white LSD
tablets, and handed them to George.

I wanted to express my gratitude for his music but I was standing next to a Beatle in a private audience and was literally speechless for once. Bear had no problem finding his voice and talked nonstop, telling George about his theories of sound, his commitment to live recording, and his belief in the transformative power of LSD and music. George listened attentively and nodded agreeably, although I had heard he preferred rehearsed music to live sound. We were standing outside a modest house on a landing in the warm California night, just hanging out. When it was time to say goodnight, George bent down and hugged Bear and hugged me. I turned my face up for a kiss and received a gentle kiss on the lips from George, the Beatle.

Grateful Maharishi

While the Grateful Dead were in LA recording *Anthem of the Sun* and performing at Shrine Auditorium, November 11, 1967, they were approached by a blonde in her early thirties who extended an invitation from Maharishi Mahesh Yogi, George Harrison's guru. They accepted, and the next day Owsley and I joined them to meet the master of Transcendental Meditation. As the passenger again, I had no idea where we were, but once again, the Hills above Hollywood—another mansion. We found the Grateful Dead in a sparsely furnished room, where we were greeted by a manicured woman in an elaborate silk sari who raised her fingers to her lips, indicating silence. I thought, what the fuck? Danny Rifkin nodded at all the shoes on the floor, and I kicked off my clogs. We were escorted into the living room and took seats on cushions on the floor. Bear fidgeted. I whispered to Sue Swanson, who gave me a look of skepticism behind her big round glasses and leaned toward me, her straight blond hair touching my face. The lady put up her finger again and spoke.

"Transcendental Meditation, or TM as we call it, is an example of mantra yoga. The student mentally repeats a series of Sanskrit words, called a mantra, for a minimum of twenty minutes every morning and evening."

We would each get our own mantra, specially selected by the great guru. It was sacred and a secret. We were not allowed to tell our mantra to anyone. We didn't have to sit in lotus position on the floor. We could recite the mantra from a chair. I liked that. I was willing. When would I get my mantra?

"The guru will see you now," she said. We all stood up. "No, the Maharishi will only give audience to the members of the band. The rest of you will receive your mantras from his assistants."

Jerry Garcia shrugged and said, "What the hell. We'll see." The band followed him through the door, leaving the rest of us in a room with no furniture.

A handsome American in loose white cotton pants and a collarless tunic tapped me gently on the shoulder. As if in a trance, I stood up and followed him into a smaller room with Indian fabrics and Oriental rugs. The incense and candles made me dizzier. Then he whispered in my ear: "Sheom."

"That's my mantra?" I asked. "Not om?"

"No," he said, "yours is different, special for you, unique," and he repeated in a whisper, "sheom."

Wow, I thought, he must know how sensitive I am to om; he must know Owsley and Melissa make OM, and I feel left out. I felt awed by the experience of being understood by a guru, even if it weren't Maharishi Mahesh Yogi himself. I repeated my mantra: sheom. I was the she, the female! Sheom: She, Owsley, and Melissa. I was an instant convert to TM.

Pigpen refused to go in, but his girl Vee went, and when she came out, she was very serious and said nothing. When everyone had gotten his mantra, and the guru's goons had gone, we began talking.

Danny asked, "What's your mantra?"

"You're not allowed to tell," I said, genuinely trying to give it a chance.

"Sheom," said Sue.

"That's mine, too," I said with disappointment.

"Yeah," said Danny. "And they asked for money."

It turned out that there were three mantras, and all of us had one of those three, except Garcia. His was something complicated, like *tara ture shvara avalokite*. Bear said the whole deal was bullshit. He refused to keep his mantra in mind for even a second and had already banished it from his consciousness.

I continued saying my mantra for years, in a chair, in bed, on a road trip, whenever I felt like it, and only recently was I told by one of my Das brother friends, Sanskrit scholar Shyamdas, that I had gotten it wrong. The word was not "she-om," but *sri-om*. There is no Sanskrit word "she-om." *Sri* means "radiance" or "to illuminate," and refers to Lakshmi, the goddess of wealth and beauty.

St. Albert and the LSD Revelation Revolution
oil painting by Alex Grey, 2006
color image in the book *Net of Being* by Alex Grey, 2012

Tablet House

We needed a place to tab the LSD, not a kitchen counter with a hand press in my Berkeley flat on Virginia Street, but a setup that would house a professional tableting press. Owsley liked the idea of hiding illicit equipment in a normal house in a normal neighborhood, and when his real estate agent friend found a house for rent in Orinda, just over the hill from Berkeley, he jumped on it. The neighborhood was suburban and the people were conservative. Perfect, according to Bear's thinking. I might have disagreed, but he didn't ask, even though we were living together.

The crew for this project included Melissa, of course, Bob Thomas, and Owsley's old Berkeley pal, Will. I was not particularly keen on any of them, but again, Owsley did not care. He arranged for the rental of five VW Bugs in different colors so we could each have our own car. Mine was green. I didn't understand why Owsley didn't rent ordinary American cars in navy, black, or gray so we would blend in. He claimed that Volkswagen Beetles were the hippest car to drive and they would throw the federal narcotic agents as such an odd choice. We were to presume that we were being followed at all times and take different routes to get to our location.

I didn't know how to drive a car with a manual shift. Owsley said, "The best way to learn how to use a clutch is to get in the car and go. This is a rental car. It does not matter if you fuck up the clutch. We'll just rent you another one. Melissa can teach you."

At rock concerts, we gave away almost the last of the LSD tabs. It was fun being generous, knowing we were about to convert the LSD we had made in Denver into hundreds of thousands of new tabs.

One by one we headed for the Tab House. I drove my VW from our house in Berkeley into Contra Costa County, through the tunnel, concentrating on the transmission, hoping I didn't stall out. There was no traffic, and I didn't have to shift at all.

My first view of the Tab House was at night. I drove the VW down the driveway and could hardly see the lights of the neighboring houses. Several acres of lawn with lush trees and bushes afforded us privacy. Melissa had arrived at the Tab House first because only she and Owsley had keys. As soon as I arrived, she made it clear that during the time we were in Orinda, she would be sharing the main bedroom with Bear. "What about Jack?" I asked, and she shrugged her shoulders, as if it were a fait accompli. Melissa was my best friend, but she didn't confide in me. I resented her, but deep down I knew my anger was misplaced.

Will helped me carry in our record collection. *The Magical Mystery Tour* had just been released, and I already knew the words to "I Am the Walrus." Coo coo ca choo.

We all had walrus impressions. Owsley grew a walruslike mustache. Will did too, but when he thought it looked incongruous with his Renaissance costume, he shaved it off. I didn't like Will, not just because he was annoying with his self-serving manner and affectations. But we had to put up with him because he was Bear's old friend and credited with getting him high. For that Bear was grateful, but I didn't see it.

Bob was the last to arrive, toting his bagpipes and sketchpad. He really didn't help with the work, but his presence as the most eccentric person there was an asset. The first thing Owsley and I did was set up the sound system. Owsley was a perfectionist about the placement of the speakers, and I was competitive in that regard.

Owsley measured the distance between the speakers for ideal placement to integrate the sound. When he thought he had gotten it right, he plugged in the cables, put on the Beatles, and turned up the volume. We went to the back of the room to listen.

"What do you think, Rhoney?" Owsley respected my opinion on sound quality. I listened carefully and smiled. Lyrics were clear, the tones rich and full, and each instrument was distinct.

We had the English LPs of *Rubber Soul* and *Sergeant Pepper*, an English EP of *Magical Mystery Tour*, and the small pressing the Beatles sent out at Christmas to thousands of their closest friends. "Lucy in the Sky with Diamonds" was released soon after the Beatles publicly announced they had taken acid. Because the initials were "LSD," many people thought Owsley played a part in the creation of the song.

"Ridiculous," he would say, but he was very pleased. He loved to share his knowledge about vinyl recording. When he took a record off the turntable, he would balance it carefully between his thumb and second finger, put it back in its sleeve, and return it to its place on the shelf like a librarian.

"Let me show you why the English pressing is better." He pointed out the thinness of the grooves compared to the American pressings. "Now you see what I mean about the difference. Technology counts. The better the raw materials, the better the product. In the United

States, we are cutting corners. We are farming out our manufacturing to save money. The English recording looks superior; it sounds superior; it is superior. I just proved it to you." Owsley had a hissy fit when we mishandled the records. If he saw fingerprints on the vinyl, someone would have to clean the record with a noxious odiferous chemical. Sometimes Owsley talked in such technical language, I did not understand what he was saying. Sometimes he uttered words like a comic-book character. He could be didactic, opinionated, a know-it-all, or just long-winded and silly.

"Recording live music is where it's at. Listen to this." He played one of his personal recordings of the Grateful Dead live. "There's feedback—an electric connection between the audience and the musicians. When it works, it's one harmonious voice vibrating in rhythm. Nobody has figured out how to record live music. We can do it! We need time, and we have to get this acid tabbed, too. LSD is part of the alchemical equation and helps the music become transformative. When are you and Melissa going to work?"

Melissa called from the kitchen, "I am making tea." Bob sat down at the table, lit up a pipe, and in his deep smoky voice, replied, "I'd like some tea, with lots of sugar, ho ho ho." He knew Owsley hated sugar and teased him by using more sugar. He passed me the pipe and I took a toke before I remembered Bob's penchant for tobacco. I almost fell over. The only thing stronger was chillum— hashish and tobacco.

Melissa bustled around the kitchen. "Anyone for food?" she asked. Food for Owsley meant meat and fat. If anyone wanted cereal for breakfast or bread or pasta for dinner, Owsley would deliver a lecture on the dangers of carbs— that the subsequent release of insulin was damaging to

all body systems, especially the cardiovascular system
as insulin regulated the production of triglycerides and
the higher the insulin, the higher the triglycerides, the
blood pressure, the weight, leading to obesity, all of which
contributed to heart disease.

"I'm not embellishing. I have not even alluded to the
pernicious effect of sugar on the liver, the pancreas, and
its causative role in diabetes," Owsley ranted. "As soon as
I uncovered this information, I stopped eating all carbs.
Are you aware that the substrate for certain cancer cells
is sugar?"

I shared his opinion that sugar was a poison and gladly
gave up my sweet tooth, a memento mori from my mother
the candy queen in opposition to my father the dentist,
who discouraged sugar and would not allow soda in the
house. My mother and father agreed on nothing. He was a
Cancer, she was a Capricorn: opposites.

Owsley cooked steaks for all of us and served them on
wooden plates that would not dull our knives. I smacked my
lips with pleasure and licked the juice running down my chin.

"Mmm, juicy. No osmosis in the frying pan." I giggled.

He looked at me, pleased, and pinched my butt as I
rose from the table, following Melissa. Owsley insisted
we change out of our street clothes before entering the
tableting room to protect the product from microscopic
bacteria, viruses, fungi, and other organic detritus.

In the changing room Melissa and I stripped off our
clothes and put on white paper coveralls, slippers on our
feet, gloves, little caps over our hair, and surgical masks.
Even so, we would still get stoned. Both of us wore
eyeglasses, and with our masks and nasal breathing, our
glasses fogged up. If we removed our glasses, we had to
change our gloves to maintain the sterile environment. If

we kept our glasses on, we couldn't see, unless we wiped each other's glasses like two mutants at play.

We worked efficiently using the finest equipment. First we checked the scale. It was kept in a tightly sealed glass case to prevent disturbances to the mechanism. We balanced the beam on the scale before weighing the glassine paper that held the binders. Even though the paper was super thin and weighed practically nothing, we still had to correct for its weight to establish the tare. Melissa put the glassine paper on one of the pans and adjusted the weight to zero, using a high-resolution balance with mechanically switched weights inside. It had two metal platforms and two pans, the right-hand pan for tare weight to weigh the container before weighing the excipients, or nonactive ingredients.

Owsley bought analytical reagent-grade materials—the purest possible—more than needed. A mixture of tribasic calcium phosphate, beta lactose, and gum tragacanth formed the adhesive powder for the LSD tablets. Melissa and I heaved the calcium phosphate onto the lab bench and opened it. The powder was dusty.

"If you breathe too hard, you disturb the material." Melissa taught me as we worked. She knew more than the professors at UC Berkeley.

"Even with a mask?"

"It's that sensitive."

"Hoohah," Bear called from the top of the stairs. "Are you ready for dispersion?"

Melissa pulled her mask down with her forearms to speak. "Come on down."

Bear and Will looked like aliens in their scrubs under the yellow light.

In a beaker, using a glass rod, Bear dissolved the LSD in methanol and food coloring. Melissa handed him the weighed calcium phosphate, and he carefully dispersed the LSD solution on the powder in another beaker. This made up 10% of the final weight of the tablets. While it dried, we weighed out the lactose and gum arabic, and Bear added these to the mixture.

"Bring me the ball mill," Bear ordered. "I want to ensure the LSD is evenly dispersed. We don't want it migrating to the surface." The ball mill whirred, the steel balls tumbled as they evenly distributed the liquid LSD throughout the powders.

Bear spread the granulation on a drying tray, covered it with a screen stretched on a frame, and placed it on a high shelf.

"Now the material must dry for the run through the press. While we wait, you can hand tabulate." He handed us each a beaker of white powder and a press with a chamber, a punch, and a pill catcher, then went upstairs to continue his research. I held the funnel as Melissa poured the compound into the tableting machine.

I realized I was starting to get high by osmosis. It was good.

I told Melissa, "I'm spacing out. Let's go listen to music for a while."

"Me too. Time to quit. Let's put the scale away first."

She morphed into Supergirl, her hair so electric that her white net cap levitated.

I stumbled out of the clean room, barely able to stand up, and in the nonsterile changing room, I peeled off my uniform and crumbled it into a ball.

Tim and Owsley had told us we had to be careful about garbage at the lab as federal narcotic agents were known to go through shit searching for incriminating evidence.

I interrupted Bear, who was absorbed in reading. "I'm

worried. Our uniforms could provide damning evidence. Do you remember the night at the Avalon Ballroom when my hands flashed under the strobe light? We had been tabbing LSD all day, and you explained that the piezoelectricity of LSD caused the luminescence. What if our uniforms flash the same way?"

Bear looked up from his book and stared at me before answering.

"You sure are paranoid, but to reassure you, I will tell you that many compounds give off energy in the form of light waves that fire under specific light spectrums. Detergents is one. If you're still paranoid, wrap your uniform in plastic."

Bob was sitting at the table, rolling his smoking herbs—tobacco, coltsfoot, and reefer. "Yellow American glass of the eighteenth and nineteenth centuries, known as Vaseline glass, flashes under fluorescent light," he added.

"It contains uranium salts, and it glows under black light or ultraviolet light but not under fluorescent light," said Bear. "Cool."

Bob's teeth were stained from tea and smoke. When I looked at him, I'd rather not smoke.

Owsley turned to Melissa and me.

We were his golden girls—our bodies shaped by ballet, our eyes like dark saucers from the pupillary effect of LSD on the autonomic nervous system.

He waved a yellow pad and poked it with his finger. "Melissa, look at this calculation. I don't like it. We're getting 67% yield. I want one gram of lysergic acid monohydrate in for one gram of LSD tartrate out."

They walked together to the bedroom, Bear and she voluble in the language of physical chemistry, familiar to them but foreign to me. It gave me the blues.

I headed for the living room and selected a record
of Indian music—Ali Akbar Khan on sarod and Ravi
Shankar playing sitar. The drummer was Allah Rakha,
the master. The sound rolled off the drum like a hollow
evocation. The smaller drum had a tune like a melody and
the larger drum was deep and resonant. I got the rhythm,
1234, 1234, 1234, 1234—fast tintal, as far away from the
blues as you can get.

The next morning, Owsley burst into the kitchen in a fit
of bad temper. While he had been at the Valley Street
house in Berkeley retrieving something he had forgotten,
Tim had phoned and warned him that our Orinda lab
was hot and he'd better stay clear of the place. We all
started talking at once, our voices rising in panic.

"What exactly did Tim say?" I shouted above the others.

Bear looked at all of us before he spoke. "He says stop the
work! The number of agents around his house on Hopkins
Street has more than doubled."

There was silence and Bear continued.

"Tim is paranoid. He raises suspicion. He was followed
from Nurnberg Scientific buying chloroform and acetone,
standard solvents. The guy behind the counter ratted on
him. Never in all my dealings as head of Bear Research
did I have this problem."

I jumped up. "I trust Tim. I believe him. If he says
abandon the work and get out, we should listen."

Melissa put her hand on my shoulder and gently
pushed me down. "Let Bear finish."

"Tim plans to fly to LA. He intends to be at Al
Mathews's law office when the Feds come for him."

Owsley was chewing his hand. "Tim says one of us was followed here and the Feds have our address. They may already have a search warrant." He crossed and uncrossed his legs, unconsciously moving his balls out of the way with his hand.

"Nobody's been following me lately," Melissa offered.

Will chortled. "Nobody can follow you."

The tension broke and we laughed.

"Maybe there's an informer," I said quietly, but everybody heard me.

"Rhoney, I trust all of us. I believe the narcs are bluffing. They want us to think there's a snitch. They're trying to undermine us from within. Major strategy to make a group fall apart—my grandfather taught me that. He believed that the laws of Prohibition violated the Constitution, the right of personal domain—the right to do to one's self whatever one will. The Feds are attempting to legislate morality. What we are doing is sacramental. The Bureau of Drug Abuse Control can't handle that."

We'd all heard that before. Owsley seemed to be talking to himself. He did not get it. He expected from others what he demanded of himself and assumed that his friends were like him, but many people we knew were not tightlipped. They would brag about knowing the King of LSD.

"Tim must have a reason," I confronted Owsley.

"Bah, humbug. I don't put stock in what Tim says. He's a garden variety Virgo."

No one spoke until I said, "Tim is not the frivolous type of Virgo."

"That's an understatement," Will chuckled.

"Rhoney may be right," added Melissa. "If Tim thinks we're in danger, we should take him seriously."

Bear stood up. "The question is: Do we finish, or do we let them stop us? The large batch is almost dry and ready for pressing."

"Perhaps we can work faster. A couple more days . . ." Melissa was improvising. "We've got it down."

"I think we should move out," I declared. "There are five of us and we each have a car. Let's start another lab in a safer place."

Bear looked agitated.

"Get real, Rhoney. To move the lab, we need a truck, not VW Bugs."

I wouldn't let it go. "We've hauled sound equipment when the white Dodge wasn't there.

"The glassware is fragile. Everything must be carefully wrapped. The boards cannot be moved. We are too close to finishing."

Melissa backed down. "Let's work together and finish quickly."

Owsley glowed. "The material is almost dry."

Bob was conciliatory. "Whatever you say sounds good to me."

Something switched inside me. I was mad at Owsley. I was mad at everyone. I believed Tim. We should get out.

Will affected his fake English accent. "Ta ta. I'm off to Berkeley to meet Donna." No one laughed.

Donna! She was a sexy chick who posed nude for posters. Bear had the hots for her, but she turned out to be a speed freak and he dropped her. I wondered what Will was doing with Donna.

Bear cautioned, "Watch out for that one, Willy."

Melissa turned to me. "Want to get back to work?"

We gowned up before entering the clean room. The door was slightly ajar. I thought we had closed it. I looked at the stack of LSD tablets, and the size seemed diminished. I had remembered having more tabs. Perhaps I was paranoid. Then I saw the scale sitting out of its case, and I knew for sure we had put it away.

We called Bear, and he examined the scale with a jeweler's loupe, finding specks of dust in the mechanism.

"This is a precision instrument and must be kept in its case. I thought everyone working here knew that."

Bear cleaned the scale, placed it in its case, and stored it on the shelf. Melissa and I added new mixture to the hand press and churned out tablets, working steadily. After a while, I felt too stoned to continue.

"Let's take a break and go upstairs," Melissa said.

Bear was reading, and I interrupted him.

"Humph," he muttered and put down his book.

"I don't want to be a tattletale, but I think Will is stealing acid."

Bear was silent. He finally replied. "So what if Will is stealing acid?"

I slammed the back door and went outside to sit like a fool on the hill that sloped up behind the house. The San Francisco fog was hiding the top branches of the trees.

I considered my choices. I could bolt and save myself, but instead I put out my cigarette, went back inside, and rejoined my friends, my family. Melissa was washing dishes. I picked up the towel and dried.

Guests at the Emperor's Breakfast

We were seated at the kitchen table drinking coffee. There was a great crashing sound, and I felt a gust of cold on my back. I turned my head and gasped. Three men with guns drawn leaped through the window. There was shattered glass on me and all over the table and the kitchen floor.

A gun was staring at me. I heard smashing from below, and more men bounded up from the stairs with their guns pointing at us. Six men surrounded our table.

In a calm voice, Owsley asked, "Do you have a search warrant?"

Immediately, an envelope was handed to Owsley.

He unfolded the document and read aloud, "December 21, 1967, 69 La Espinal Street, Orinda, California." Owsley looked up at the winded enforcer.

"This is a legitimate search warrant. How did you manage to find this place?"

"We have informants."

Another narc in a thermal vest with binoculars draped around his neck seemed familiar with the layout of the house.

I shook my head back and forth. I could not find my voice.

Soon more agents arrived. Twelve in all. There were federal and state enforcement officials and even local cops. They searched our house. Nothing was off limits with a federal search warrant. Until the search was complete, they would not let us move or make a phone call.

Owsley crumbled, his judgment wrong. Someone he had chosen had betrayed him. Someone in his intimate circle had made him vulnerable to law enforcement. Now he was hunched on the couch in handcuffs.

The phone rang and the narc in the dark suit answered the phone. I was praying it was Tim calling and he would figure out that we were under arrest and get a lawyer on the case immediately. "Owsley is busy right now." The narc held up the phone and we heard the disconnection sound.

We were handcuffed and led out to the police cars. I was wearing my bear fur vest; Melissa had on her Guatemalan tribal dress. At the police station a female matron patted us down and put us in a cell with bunk beds and a toilet in the middle of the floor. Light glared from a bare bulb in the ceiling. The mattresses sagged. We spent the night in the Contra Costa County jail, but we did not sleep.

The next day, December 22, we were taken by police car to the Courthouse in Oakland and appeared before US Commissioner Harold Jewitt for the Northern District of California. The charge was conspiracy to illegally manufacture controlled drugs; however, the US Attorney announced he was reassessing the charges and adding sale of illegal drugs. Our lawyer protested, and the original charge remained. We were each released on $5,000 cash bond. Federal, state, and local officials claimed our arrest was the biggest LSD arrest in history and their haul of drugs was worth nearly $11 million.

Up Against the Wall

Thank God for the Hell's Angels.

After the police spent two days overturning furniture and sweeping books off their shelves, they wrapped the house in yellow crime scene tape and stapled some edict to our door, which they padlocked. Terry the Tramp and his Hell's Angel brother Little George broke in and recovered Bear's cache of cash and his stash. I still don't know where it was hidden.

Owsley's legal team was headed by Al Matthews, his long-time attorney in LA. Bear was now spending most of his time poring over law books that he bought at the Boalt Law School bookstore in Berkeley. Books covered the kitchen table; books sat on the chairs. Some had strips of paper serving as markers. Law cases with similar scenarios to ours were of particular interest. The Grand Jury indictment was scheduled for January 11, 1968.

"The purpose of a grand jury," explained Owsley, "is to review the evidence and decide whether there is probable cause to charge the victim with the crime. This is our first shot at knocking down their case. The Feds have to show sufficient cause to indict us."

"What about the State? State narcs were at the bust."

"This is a federal bust, Rhoney, not a state bust, and federal law takes precedence over state law, according to the supremacy clause, Article VI, Clause 2 of the United States Constitution." Owsley read out of a heavy book:

"This Constitution and the Laws of the United States which shall be made in pursuance thereof; and all treaties made, or which shall be made, under the authority of the United States, shall be the supreme law of the land; and the judges in every state shall be bound thereby, any thing in the Constitution or law of any state to the contrary notwithstanding."

I listened automatically, absorbing his opinion. "What you read says the states must concur with federal law, that they are bound by the authority of the United States law," I parroted back with his same confidence.

Owsley continued.

"All persons born or naturalized in the United States, and subject to the jurisdiction thereof, are citizens of the United States and of the state wherein they reside. No state shall make or enforce any law which shall abridge the privileges or immunities of citizens of the United States; nor shall any state deprive any person of life, liberty, or property without due process of law; nor deny to any person within its jurisdiction the equal protection of the laws."

Owsley's great-great-grandfather had come to America on the fucking Mayflower. His grandfather had been governor and United States senator from Kentucky. His godfather had served as a Supreme Court Justice

on the Warren Bench. Owsley had such faith in the
fairness of the United States Constitution, the document
illuminati, that he believed the spirit of his American
forefathers would protect his individual rights.

"You've heard of 'due process'?" he asked me.

"Yes," I chimed in. "I took Constitutional Law at
Mount Holyoke." His eyes returned to the book.

"No state shall deny any person the right to life, liberty,
and property, and the basic rights we have as citizens
of the United States. It's the American Magna Carta.
The due process clause of the Fourteenth Amendment
guarantees that the Bill of Rights is applied to the states.
No state law can take away individual rights."

"That means the state of California can't indict us?"
My words sounded like a question. I really didn't have
that confidence. Deep down, I knew we were doomed. My
intuition was raising her voice.

Bear lit the mint leaves in his pipe. His pot pouch was
on the table. I sat down and pulled out a bud of sinsemilla
and chanticleers and began the ritual of rolling a joint, my
hands shaky.

"Will the Feds indict me?"

"The Fifth Amendment requires a grand jury
indictment for federal criminal charges. If we can show
that you and Melissa were just chicks hanging out at the
place, you won't be indicted."

"Bear, we were making LSD."

His face became expressionless. Then he returned to
his book, reading to himself.

What did this all mean? Had we suffered bad karma?
My parents must have heard about it, but I wasn't going
to call and ask.

Bear looked up over his glasses. "You and Melissa will not go to jail because I am going to take the rap." He went back to his reading.

Before the Grand Jury indictment, the federal government dropped the charges against Melissa and me. We were free. On January 11, 1968, Owsley went to court while we waited together at the kitchen table at Valley Street.

The phone rang. Melissa grabbed it.

"It's Owsley," she said. "He's been indicted for conspiracy to manufacture LSD."

First artwork for *Live/Dead* album cover by Bob Thomas

Carousel Ballroom

In early 1968, there were three places in San Francisco for rock'n'roll shows: Winterland, the Fillmore, and the Avalon. Chet Helms, a sweet man and a great hippie, ran the Avalon. His "anything goes" way of doing business was tenuous, and undercover narcs got into the hall, making the place unsafe for the regulars. He was going broke, but he was a friend. Bill Graham ran Winterland and the Fillmore. He did not like Owsley or LSD.

Owsley and Bill Graham had a nasty encounter at the Fillmore as we were leaving a gig one night. Bill Graham popped out of the crowd and stood in front of Owsley at the bottom of the stairs. We were very high, and he had bad vibes.

"Did you buy a ticket?" he asked accusingly, pointing his finger at Bear's chest. "You came to the show, you bring her, think you're better than everybody else!" Then he launched into a tirade demanding "his" money. His voice was raised and his yellow face pinched up. Bear was tottering on the steps. I got paranoid.

Bear reached into his pocket, pulled out hundred-dollar bills and fanned them in front of Bill Graham's big nose just as Jack showed up with Melissa on his arm. Bill Graham adored Jack and had managed the Jefferson Airplane before an amiable split a few months earlier.

"Good evening," Jack drawled like some Viking prince. "Is there a problem?"

Bill Graham shook his head and walked away. It was like smoke hanging over the O.K. Corral.

At that time, the Carousel Ballroom was not a regular venue for rock 'n' roll. It had been a popular Irish dance hall called El Patio in the 1950s. It was a real ballroom, not just a space converted into a dance hall, or a former ice-skating rink, like Winterland. The landlord, Bill Fuller, was a tough Irish bloke from County Kerry who owned twenty-three dance halls around the world. He had enough chutzpah to introduce Irish dancing to Las Vegas. He was an entrepreneur and street smart. Apparently, renting the Carousel to hippies was fine with him.

Bear's birthday, January 19, was looming and there were no plans to celebrate, but when he heard that the Grateful Dead management had rented the Carousel Ballroom for a performance on January 17, he perked up. What better way to change the vibe than to throw a party open to all? January 17 was Benjamin Franklin's birthday. Close enough.

Bear and the quippies, Ramrod and Hagen, moved sound equipment from our home in Berkeley and Bear's storage garage. Before the birthday concert began, I walked onto the stage and among the busy quippies and crew was my old flame from UC Berkeley days, Jerry Abrams. He was setting up a screen at the back of the upstage area for the light show. It was his lighting company, Headlights, doing the gig. He swooped me into his big arms and gave me a kiss.

"I see you've become a hippie. Welcome to the psychedelic revolution," I joked to him. Suddenly, Bear appeared carrying in a heavy amplifier. He took an immediate dislike to Jerry Abrams.

"If you cannot stay out of the way of the sound equipment, you will be banned from the stage," he instructed Jerry Abrams, as if that were the issue.

Bear was jealous and I was scared. Abrams stopped smiling and returned to setting up his light show. The audience filled the floor and the band began to play, but I couldn't even get into the music. When Bear found me, I was sitting backstage sulking. He dragged me to the dance floor, and we danced and smiled again.

KMPX, the first FM radio station to play the new psychedelic rock, was on Green Street in San Francisco, and Tom Donahue, the main DJ, known as Big Daddy, was innovative and iconoclastic; Tony Bigg the Pig, his assistant, was handsome and a chick magnet. Late one night, Bear and I went to North Beach to the KMPX studio before Big Daddy's overnight shift. We walked through dark hallways to the broadcast room, the only cubicle lit up, and by the end of the evening, KMPX was making a live broadcast of the Grateful Dead on Valentine's Day at the Carousel Ballroom with the Berkeley band Country Joe and the Fish as the opening act.

As Valentine's Day began, the Grateful Dead quippies brought the equipment to the Carousel and stacked the stage with tie-dye speakers and amplifiers custom designed by Bear. We went back to Berkeley to dress for the show. Bear embraced me from behind and whispered in my ear.

"Let's make love, valentine."

"A quickie," I uttered amorously, "we don't want to be late."

Nothing took precedence over sex.

Of course, we were late getting to the Carousel and the band was irked.

"You're late!" Garcia shouted when we arrived.

We smiled and Bear took his place at the sound board. I was wearing boots and a miniskirt with a wolf's tail in my hair.

From the very first note, the sound was clear and balanced. At break, Phil announced his praise for the venue and the sound. After the show, members of the Grateful Dead, Quicksilver, the Jefferson Airplane, and Big Brother spontaneously met in the back room and discussed renting the Carousel and running it as their own clubhouse. The dressing room was plush with carpeting and velvet settees and armchairs.

Garcia spoke. "For the Carousel to work, the bands have to play for free."

A raucous discussion ensued. "We play for free," Jerry repeated. "The Carousel collects the take at the end of the gig."

Ron Polte, manager for Quicksilver Messenger Service, was sitting next to Bear, mooching pot from him and bogarting the joint. He could make smoking pot seem greedy. Bear liked to share and frowned.

"Quicksilver's in!"

Bear smiled.

Bill Thompson, the Jefferson Airplane's manager, reminded everyone that the Airplane was preparing for their first European tour, and he would not have time to help with the Carousel.

"That's okay," Jerry reassured him. "We'll get a management team."

Jack Casady slouched on the couch with his arm around Melissa. "We'll play for free whenever we're in town. That's what counts." He rolled his eyes behind his rose-colored glasses.

"House bands," I blurted out. "Like in the jazz age—
Duke Ellington at the Cotton Club."

"No, Rhoney," Jerry corrected me. "Those bands
were paid."

Janis interrupted. "Albert won't let us play for free,
but I'll be hanging out here. Don't you worry. Me and
my Southern buddies. Right, Pigboy?" she said. "Have
y'all met my friend, Elvin Bishop? He's a real Southern
gentleman and plays a mean guitar."

He wore overalls and a straw cowboy hat and spoke
with a Southern twang. "Thanks for the nice review,
darling." She tousled his hair and took a slug from the
flask of Southern Comfort they were sharing.

Bear gave her a disapproving look because of his
hatred of alcohol, then spoke to his needs. "If we lease
the Carousel, I can build an electronics shop here. I need
a place to work on the sound system and the guitars. Let's
show Bill Graham," Bear continued. "He treats Chet
Helms like shit. He makes fun of the Avalon because it's
losing money. He won't even let us keep equipment at
the Fillmore." Bear paused to get his breath to continue
the long list of grievances he held toward Bill Graham.
"He makes us pay even when he uses our microphones
and amplifiers."

Ramrod added to the conversation. "He charges us
and we carry the equipment."

"Tear down the Fillmore," said one of the quippies.

"Gas Winterland," declared another loudmouth.

"Bill Graham's trip is money," I said.

"He's a small-minded asshole," Bear grunted.

"Fuck Bill Graham," Hagen bellowed.

"Dose Bill Graham," Ramrod decreed.

"Lease the Carousel," I exclaimed with exhilaration.

The location of the Carousel Ballroom was perfect, on the seedier side of San Francisco, close to the Mission, where loud rock 'n' roll would bother no one.

"The landlord lives in Ireland," Rock, ever managerial, declared.

"An absentee landlord. That's the best kind," I shared.

"Who's in charge?" Ramrod questioned, looking at Garcia.

"I am not the leader," Garcia responded. "We need a business team, and I want no part of it."

That ended the meeting.

A group of us went to Original Joe's and Bear paid for everyone. We did nothing but talk about leasing the Carousel. Bear did not once mention his law case.

As we were driving back to Berkeley, he said, "Rhoney, you should do business. You'd be good at business. You're a natural!" He laughed. "You're Jewish."

I was taken aback, not at the racist and sexist remark, but because he was saying he didn't want me on his sound team. That hurt.

He said, "Rhoney, I need sound engineering. You have no technical training. *I* don't even have the skills we need."

It was four in the morning when we parked in front of our home and walked up the cobblestone path to the Valley Street house. I felt dejected. I wanted to spend every moment of my life with Bear, but he did not reciprocate. He opened the door, and Screech did not fly down from the beam and land on his head. Ever since the bust, the owl had been acting weird. I sat down at the stone bench by the fireplace, and Bear lit a fire. The amber eyes of the owl andirons glowed with the flames. I felt stuck at the Valley Street house. Most of my friends had left Berkeley, but not us. In Berkeley, narcs followed us and even parked near our house, slumped in their cars as if they were invisible. I wished Bear would move to Marin, but he would not consider my needs or feelings, except during sex.

I rubbed his back as he crouched in front of the fire. "Shall I put on *Sgt. Pepper's*?" I asked.

"Yes," was the answer.

He watched me as I put the LP on the turntable without touching the vinyl, dramatically imitating his fastidious style.

The Beatles used wah-wah pedals and fuzz boxes, and the tracks were recorded at various speeds. The effect was innovative and psychedelic, and listening, I understood how music could be a power for transformation. I thought, if I couldn't be part of Bear's sound crew, I'd die.

At the next meeting at the Carousel, Rock brought Ron Rakow, who volunteered to be the business manager. He had been hanging around the Grateful Dead, looking for an in. He had loaned the Grateful Dead money and never asked for it back. He was flashy. Like me, he was a Jew from the East Coast with an upper-middle-class family. He wanted to form a new company, separate from the Grateful Dead, that would manage the business of the Carousel. This would free the Grateful Dead from liability, and as CEO, he would obtain the lease. We were thrilled with his business acumen and liked the way he strutted around the darkened Carousel as if he owned the place. He immediately located Bill Fuller, the landlord from Ireland, and successfully negotiated a lease. Within days, Bear moved all his equipment into the Carousel, and the new team planned an opening night for March 15, 1968, when the Jefferson Airplane and the Dead were both in town.

Bear found joy engineering the sound system for the Carousel. His right to travel out of the jurisdiction of his arrest had been revoked, so he could not go on the road with the Grateful Dead, but he could forget about his legal problems in the music.

With the business aspect of the Carousel under control, I assumed I was part of the sound crew and listened carefully to Bear's rambling.

"The musicians must hear themselves, and they must hear the house mix. We will build the best sound system for the musicians at the Carousel, with monitors that have the same quality as the house speakers."

"Are you going to record the shows?" I asked.

"Of course," Bear responded.

"Let's show Bill Graham a dance hall can be run out of love instead of greed."

"Never happen, unless he's dosed." Bear shook his head.

I assisted Ramrod with arranging the stage. "How do you like the way Rakow got that deal done?" I asked him.

"He's a crafty little Jew," Ramrod answered with a smile, looking into my eyes with his large blue ones. "Yeah. I like it." He never said "yes," always "yeah." He spoke like a cowboy, out of the corner of his mouth, in short sentences, curling his lips inward, but he looked at you when he talked, unlike Bear, who hardly ever met you with his eyes.

"Where is Bear?" I asked. Ramrod shrugged. I figured Bear must be fucking somebody in a closet somewhere.

I looked in the kitchen. The Carousel Ballroom had a professional kitchen, with stainless steel sinks, a huge stove, and a big grill with a hood and fan.

"Hoohah," I called expecting Bear's echo, but Annie Corson, the cook at the Jefferson Airplane house, stepped out from behind the freezer.

"I love this kitchen. Who knew?" Annie was wearing a long peasant skirt, her hair pulled back neatly with a scarf. "A six-burner with a hood! This is too much!" She volunteered to take over the management of the kitchen.

"We'll need a kitchen crew," I thought out loud, anticipating cost. Then I realized we family members were finding our places, like a game of musical chairs. She was in the right place at the right time.

Betty Cantor talked her way into the job of serving hot dogs. She had her eyes on Bob Matthews in the sound booth. She was high maintenance, gorgeous, and intelligent. With a name like Cantor, she must have some Jewishness in her. All of a sudden I was jealous and insecure.

Jonathan Reister was someone's friend and a real rodeo cowboy. He was a quick talker and easy on the eyes. He and I bonded on the spot in Rakow's office.

His feet were up on Rakow's desk, his rattlesnake leather cowboy boots beside a black 1950s telephone. Rakow had the telephone to his ear.

Jonathan gave advice with authority. "Man, you gotta talk to these dudes right. Let 'em know we take no nonsense and we pay in cash."

Rakow pointed at Jonathan's boots. "I want those!"

I got up from the couch and felt the skin. It had texture. "These are real cowboy boots." Jonathan kicked them off. He was wearing expensive wool socks. I felt the inside of the boot—soft leather.

"What size are you?" Jonathan asked running his fingers through his curly copper hair.

"I wear size 6," I said.

"Size 6, such small feet," he cooed to me. "Size 12 for me."

Jonathan placed an even larger order. Weir was in. Susila Kreutzmann made it clear she had to have her Texas cowgirl boots.

Bear gave his opinion. "I'd rather go barefoot."

Rakow said, "Give me the bill for our new company, Triad. Isn't that clever? Three to represent the three bands supporting the Carousel: the Dead, the Quick, and the Airplane."

I thought, why isn't he worried about money? Who was going to pay for cowboy boots? There was no cash flow, and already there were expenses.

Bear's sound equipment filled the stage and the sound booth and the makeshift shop in the balcony. He rejected the modern solid-state equipment in favor of heavy tubes. Tubes were superior, he claimed, providing the most power, and power was the driving force of rock 'n' roll. Even with distortion, the sound was saturated and steady. His sound booth had a board, an oscilloscope, and a tape recorder, and he set up a workbench where he could solder. His goal was to modify the sound equipment with state-of-the-art electronics using tubes and modern Mylar. He was opening up all the equipment, tearing out the old resistors and capacitors and replacing them with new components. He told me everything had to be unsoldered and resoldered.

I drove to the Peninsula to pick up an order at Hewlett-Packard. He only paid in cash, so I carried a paper bag of hundred-dollar bills. The drive was so monotonous, I almost fell asleep on the road. Carefully, I carried a wrapped package of precision parts to his shop upstairs at the Carousel, but he wasn't there. I assumed he was out fucking some chick. He returned with Melissa. He leaned down to suck my nipple when she wasn't looking, took the package, dumped all the contents into a big stack on his workbench, and with his clawlike fingers pulled out the part he wanted.

I heard a grunt. "Ground wire," he said.

He set up two wires in a vise to teach us how to solder. He took a soldering iron torch and turned the valve to ignite the tip. A bright orange flame burst forth. He adjusted the oxygen content of the flame until it turned electric blue.

"Watch out," he cried over the hissing jet as I moved closer to see this fabulous light. "A blue flame is the hottest flame and has a range far greater than what you can see."

Holding the solder in one hand and the soldering iron in the other, he showed us how the solder melted and fused the two metals. Melissa picked up the soldering iron and fused the wire to a jack on her first try.

Then it was my turn. My heart beat wildly. I became irrational with anxiety.

"Aren't you afraid of burning your hair?" I was attempting to cop out. Bear and Melissa looked at me.

I was acting crazy. "Oh, that's right! Melissa's a Leo. She *is* fire. Leo, a fire sign, the sun, the king beast of the jungle, the natural leader, the best sign." I bitched, "I'm a measly Virgo, an earth sign—a receptive sign. What do I have to do with fire?"

Bear said, "Hey, Rhoney, if Melissa can do it, you can too. Besides, your hands are small."

Small and shaking, I thought.

I took the iron in my right hand and the solder in my left, but the solder fizzled and hardened and did not melt.

Bear criticized. "You're too aggressive. You didn't hold the flame at the right distance."

Bear and Melissa were laughing together over a blue soldering flame, and I walked out of the shop. Screw you, I thought. I love you, but you're not loyal.

On the stage, Ramrod and Rex had lined up the amps and were unscrewing the casings with a long automatic screwdriver. I tried it and made them laugh out loud. Betty and Matthews sorted the cables, opening the connectors to see if anything needed soldering. Ramrod smiled his wry boyish smile at me. Could I find a role with the Grateful Dead family? Not soldering, that was clear.

The dance floor was solid hardwood but rough. Bear said it was only rough from disuse, and the more people who danced on it, the more polished it would get, like an object develops a patina. He went on and on, irritating everyone, until Rakow said, "It's rough. We're polishing it. I'm hiring a crew."

Bear fussed and said, "Unnecessary," but he was overruled.

Rakow hired a crew, and although they were mainly kids from the street and young runaways from home, we had to pay them. Then there was the discussion about whether the stage should be moved.

"Waste of money," Bear muttered. I agreed. The acoustics were good everywhere in the hall. But Rakow insisted we move the stage and hired carpenters, and that increased the payroll. Later it turned out that the carpenter was Rakow's black chick's brother. He was a great carpenter, always on hand at the Carousel, and even helped Bear build the electronics workshop.

"What are we going to put on the marquee?" I asked. The Carousel had a real marquee like an authentic movie theater. Everyone thought we should use it to advertise the upcoming events, but I said, "No! We should be different and not advertise. Let's put up pithy sayings—like 'Psychedelics Rock' or 'Be Here Now' or 'Love One Another' or 'Go with the Flow' or 'Have Fun' or 'Peace'—anything to make a statement."

"How about 'Eat Cunt'?" one of the quippies offered.

"Ha, ha," I responded.

Another time, the discussion was about the cost of tickets. If it were up to Danny Rifkin, admission would be free.

"No way. We are running a ballroom, not a community center," said Rakow stepping in. "We'll charge the same as Bill Graham."

"One stipulation: all musicians get in free," said Garcia.

When Emmett Grogan, head of the Diggers, heard that musicians got in for nothing, he demanded equal treatment for the poor. He was a former actor with the San Francisco Mime Troupe and cocky, a people magnet. He thought nothing of stealing from the rich to feed the poor. I could see our profit margin disappearing.

Garcia asked, "Who wants to man the ticket booth?" A mistake, asking for volunteers for that job.

"We do!" Connie and Sue Swanson piped up, waving their hands and jumping up and down.

Garcia couldn't say no to Swanson with her plain good looks and honesty. Mistake #2. Sue whispered to me in a singsong voice, "We control who gets in."

"Good for you," I sang back.

Vibrating with joy, her breasts bounced under her white T-shirt, and I could see the dark aureoles of her nipples. She put her finger to her lips and whispered, "I'm pregnant!"

"Who's the father?" I mouthed.

Ron Rakow was on the telephone at his desk. She pointed at him.

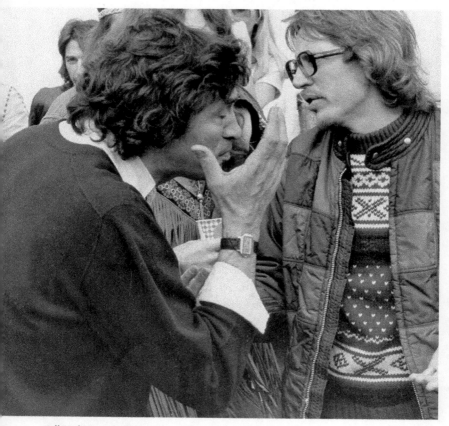

Bill Graham and Bill Thompson, manager of The Jefferson Airplane   © *Alvan Meyerowitz*

Not About Cream

Cream was coming to town, performing five nights at Winterland and the Fillmore West. Cream was the hottest band in the world, and Bear wished they would play through his sound system, but their contract with Bill Graham prohibited them from playing at the Carousel Ballroom.

Bear poked the newspaper and passed me a joint.

"The San Francisco Ballet will be in town. I bet Jack Bruce likes ballet. He is a classically trained musician. Let's get tickets and invite Jack Bruce and his wife. I want to talk to him about customizing his bass."

"Oh, Bear, how fabulous!" I hugged him and then put on *Fresh Cream*, Cream's first record, released in the UK in December, 1966. Bear preferred the mono version. For him, purity was greater in mono sound—a single audio signal sent to more than one speaker with all speakers reproducing the same sound, no splitting.

I danced my way back to the kitchen, singing "I feel free," my bare breasts jiggling as I moved.

"I want to meet Jack Bruce's wife. I read somewhere that she wrote the words to 'Sleepy Time Time.'"

"'Work only maybe, life is a joy.'" Bear intoned with his finger in the air. "Whoever wrote those lyrics needs to take more acid."

I had to laugh. We had heard that Jack Bruce's wife never took LSD, so Owsley was obsessed with turning her on. Her lyrics were a bit simple, but I admired the fact

that she got to cowrite with Cream. I had filled several
notebooks with my attempts at poetry.

"If only we could make more acid." Bear scowled,
cradling his head in his hands. The bust had brought
us down.

Bear bought four tickets for the San Francisco Ballet in
advance. We were double dating with Jack Bruce and his
wife, Janet Godfrey! All I could think about was what to
wear. Bear said the San Francisco Ballet was conservative
and not to dress in a costume. I rushed to my closet and
tried on black satin bell-bottoms. Too tight. I threw the
pants on the floor and pulled out a pair in black velvet, but
I couldn't find a top. I finally chose a black paisley dress
with bat sleeves and a décolleté neckline, and two-toned
high heels with a T-strap. Fuck me pumps, we called them.

When the evening arrived, we were in the marble foyer
of the San Francisco Opera House when we spotted the
royal couple of rock 'n' roll walking through the crowd. I
was amazed to see that Jack Bruce's wife was dressed in a
conservative wool suit. We introduced ourselves, and Owsley
handed us each our ticket. As Janet got hers, Bear started his
rap abut the benefits of the psychedelic experience.

Jack turned to me and asked, "Is he always so insistent
on having the last word?"

I regretfully nodded yes and smiled.

When the ballet began, we were riveted on the
performance. Bear was so enraptured that he uttered little
cries of delight, oohs and ahs of admiration, and focused
on the dancers. The ballet was breathtaking, and we
caught his enthusiasm. For those moments we were bound
by the same movements and rhythms. At intermission
Bear looked around the theater for someone he knew. He
wanted to go backstage and turn the dancers on to LSD.

I was so distracted sitting next to Jack Bruce. I paid far too much attention to him, touching his forest green velvet jacket, noticing the collarless shirt, a style like a parson's frock. His page-boy haircut and English schoolboy accent, polite manners, soft voice, and earnest way of listening made me feel I was sitting with Prince Charming.

"Let's go to Original Joe's," Bear said after the final grand pas. That was our custom. The Grateful Dead, the Jefferson Airplane, and our friends often ended the evening at OJ's. No matter how high we were on LSD, a steak at OJ's was a ritual. Although the restaurant was located in the Tenderloin, the down-and-out section of San Francisco, it was comfortable, with wood paneling, leather banquettes, and a curved wooden bar with high leather chairs that swiveled. The food was delicious.

"Good evening, sir," said the old guy behind the bar. We sat on the red leather stools and the old guy showed Bear a platter with a two-and-a-half-inch-thick prime rib.

"Look at that marbling! Oh, la, la." He licked his lips and smiled his approval. Jack Bruce rolled his eyes.

Janet, which she pronounced more like Janette or Jeanette, was very proper and polite, and I recall her drinking a cocktail at Original Joe's, pursing her lips at the sourness. Bear joked that if she took LSD, her lips would smile. I think he was really disappointed that he could not convince her of the LSD miracles so close at hand.

We rapped about the ecstasy of live recordings, agreeing with Jack Bruce that live recordings were the only way to go. When Cream released *Wheels of Fire* in August of 1968, much of it recorded live at Winterland and the Fillmore, we were certain it was inspired by our conversation.

The Jefferson Airplane and the Grateful Dead opened

the Carousel Ballroom to a sold-out crowd, March 15, 16, and 17, 1968.

Bear set up spiked Kool-Aid backstage, and we were all high before the show even started, which delayed the show until the audience was hissing and screaming and demanding that a band start playing. The Jefferson Airplane went on first. While the Airplane was playing, Bear was still working on the Dead's electronics, running back and forth from the sound booth to the stage, and I followed. He wound his way through the audience, the pack of dancers parting like the Red Sea. Everyone knew who he was, and if you asked him for acid, he would give you a dose. I took some more under my tongue. All the way to the stage, we stopped and got people high. Bear wore a leather vest with a tight tie-dye short-sleeve T-shirt that showed off his biceps. My dress swirled as I hurried after Bear across the dance floor, concentrating like Bear on the job at hand.

To me, Grace sounded like she was screaming. Jorma and Jack were smiling as they played. Everybody was psychedelic. When the Airplane stopped, Bear still had not finished setting up the Dead's equipment, and I started to worry.

I wondered, why couldn't he be on time? Why did his drive for perfection cause so many problems? Finally, the Grateful Dead went on, but Bear was still fiddling with the equipment as the band began to play. He moved between the drummers to reposition the mics. Nothing could distract the band once they started, but I felt in the way. I had to stop following him around. Maybe that's what he wanted.

I made my way back into the house and through the crowd. Up front were the wild-eyed guitar fanatics, then a more mellow group of hippies, smoking pot and smiling. The music was louder than I thought, which I learned when I tried to talk. On the side were the spinners, girls in long colorful skirts interpretatively dancing to the music, never stopping their motion.

I went up to the balcony, past the light show that was made by people using overhead projectors, color wheels, liquid slides, and eyedroppers of colorful oils to project psychedelic images on the screen above the stage. I found the most remote seat in the house, an old sofa, and sat beside a stoned hippie who looked like a garden troll. I smiled despite myself. The sound was wonderful. The air was filled with pot smoke and the scent of patchouli oil and roses. The music filled the enclosed space with transformative energy and even I was feeling it. Success!

"Rules? Piss on your fucking rules!" *

When Bear wasn't at the Carousel, he was working on his law case. Despite the fact that he had money and could hire the most prestigious lawyers, he stuck with Al Matthews in LA out of loyalty and the security of Al's affection for him. Al had hired several lawyers, but they all seemed wimpy. When Bear talked to them on the phone, he told them the arguments to make rather than the other way around.

We were sitting at the kitchen table on Valley Street in Berkeley. The following day was Bear's first hearing at the Ninth Circuit Court of Appeals in San Francisco, and once again he was on the phone with his lawyers. I heard him say, "The LSD the Feds confiscated was for my personal use."

When he hung up, I put in my two cents. "Bear, are you for real? You were found with more than a million dollars worth of LSD. How can you say it was for personal use?"

*Ken Kesey, *One Flew Over the Cuckoo's Nest*

"The lawyers agree with me. What do you know?"

Bear went into the other room and brought back a heavy book. He thumbed through the pages. He had a photographic memory and could locate a passage in a book in an instant. When he found the passage he pointed at it with his finger.

"The Fourth Amendment—the right of privacy. My use of LSD is a privacy issue, protected under the Bill of Rights. There is a legal reason to reverse the original decision. My lawyers have legal precedent. I will win this case. If I lose at the Ninth Circuit, I will take it all the way to the Supreme Court."

"Wow, Bear, that is so extreme. What makes you think the Court will even examine your brief? Not every case gets heard by the Supreme Court. Just because your godfather was once a Supreme Court Justice—"

"Your opinion is meaningless, Rhoney. My lawyers assure me I have a shot at winning this case."

"Your lawyers just want your money. You're not going to win! You'd be better off spending your money on the Carousel."

This was our first serious disagreement.

Melissa and I accompanied Bear to the United States Court of Appeals on Seventh and Mission Streets in San Francisco. Bear was wearing a long-sleeved shirt, a leather vest, and dark pants; Melissa and I were in conservative dresses.

"Wow," I said as we approached the building, marveling at the façade that featured carved granite lions with their tongues painted red.

"Well, that's quite an omen," Bear said.

The lobby was just as imposing; the walls were different shades of marble and lined with Doric columns

and high, curved windows. The domed ceilings had round
stained-glass windows. It was surprisingly empty. As we
walked down the wide corridor, headed for the courtroom,
my heels clacked on the marble floor.

Suddenly, Bear stopped. His friend Joan Baez, her hair
cut short, was moving at a fast pace toward an exit.

"Hey, Joannie," he called to her. "What are you
doing here?"

With rage in her voice she told us that the Court had
taken her husband, David, to jail for draft dodging. Her legal
team had failed to prove that the right to refuse conscription
was a Constitutional right. Talk about bad omens.

She was outraged at the injustice. Bear spoke to
her conspiratorially, feeling she was as angry at the
interpretation of the law as he was.

"My case is built on similar precedents. The Fourth
Amendment of the Bill of Rights guarantees the right of
privacy. I have a personal right to take psychedelics. I am
harming no one."

"How dare you say that your right to take LSD is the
same as my husband's right to challenge the draft?" I
thought, oh, man, where is this going?

Bear defended LSD. "Psychedelics are extremely useful.
Very few things can reverse early imprinting, but research
has shown that psychedelics can. Research must continue,
but the government stopped all research. The Feds make
any hallucinogenic drug illegal as fast as we change the
molecule to a different psychoactive derivative. You
who talk about freedom, don't you see that government
regulation of psychedelics is a sign of an unfree society?"

She made a face.

"Bullshit." Bear was mad. "You need to hear the
Grateful Dead high on acid."

Joan Baez may have been a folk icon, but she was no friend of LSD. She was acting like a cunt, and Bear was acting like an asshole. Bear scurried off to the courtroom, disgruntled. The hearing was put over to a future date.

The next week, the Grateful Dead's management got a phone call from a representative of Joan Baez. Would the band do a benefit in support of David Harris's draft resistance efforts? Garcia was against it. He did not believe that rock'n'roll bands should take sides in the political fray, that the act of playing music was enough of a political statement. Garcia said you could make a strong case for either side; it was just a question of who was better at argument. The Grateful Dead said no, they would not do a benefit to support Joan Baez's political cause.

Photographs

Owsley at a gig   © *Alvan Meyerowitz*

Rhoney in her Berkeley apartment   © *Alvan Meyerowitz*

Kidd Candelario on the streets of Novato   © *Alvan Meyerowitz*

Backstage with Alla Rakha, Owsley and Rhoney at right   © *Jeanne Millay*

Owsley and Jerry Garcia at the airport

© Rosie McGee

Ramrod (in profile) and Rakow

© Alvan Meyerowitz

Owsley with Phil Lesh

© Alvan Meyerowitz

Bobby Weir, Frankie, and Ursula

© Alvan Meyerowitz

Jorma Kaukonen and Jack Casady onstage
© Alvan Meyerowitz

Owsley at Watkins Glen, 1973
© Blue Bailey

Owsley onstage

© Rosie McGee

Owsley at Fillmore East, February 11, 1970   © Amalie R. Rothschild

Owsley at mixing board   *Image courtesy of Owsley Stanley*

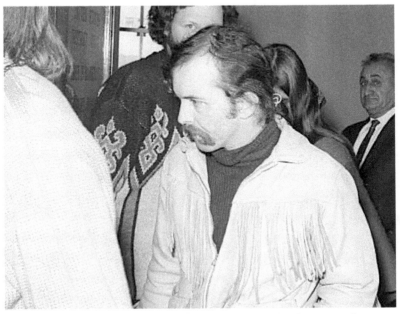

Owsley at his arraignment with federal agents, Rhoney directly behind him   © *Corbis Images*

Jack Casady with Redbird

© Alvan Meyerowitz

Gathering at Mickey Hart's ranch   © Alvan Meyerowitz

Melissa Cargill at Renaissance Pleasure Faire site

The Grateful Dead onstage at Golden Gate Park, September 28, 1974   © *Alvan Meyerowitz*

Starfinder Stanley

Starfinder with his father in New York City

Rhoney and Owsley at his home in Australia

Owsley's Winged Heart pendant, crafted in prison

Notes on a Lady.
She was a Capricorn. Jan 19.
We had the same birthday.
It must be a weird day for
being born. Edgar Allen Poe
and Robt. E. Lee and Cezanne
and Richard Lester. We had
our differences. Don't mis-
understand, I loved her – I
wanted to share what I had
found. "You've got your thing,
honey, and I've got mine",
She would say, pulling at
a bottle of Southern Comfort. But
it's all right. She was scared.
She was trying to hide. I
knew she was fighting a
phantom — one which could
dissolve in the Light. She
didn't. It was her path,

Page one of an essay on Janis Joplin, written by Owsley in prison

Owsley Runs Wild

The Jefferson Airplane, Quicksilver, and the Grateful Dead were fast becoming popular and received more and more offers to do shows out of town. Being on the road became a way of life. The Grateful Dead had developed the five-hundred-mile rule: when you're five hundred miles away on the road, you can do what you want and it ain't nobody's business.

Sometimes the chicks went with the bands, but most of the time they stayed at home. We got together in a back room at the Carousel and rolled up joints for the guys to take on the road. We piled the grass in a large bowl on the table and rolled by hand or with a rolling machine. By hand, I could roll a joint quicker, but it was always fat in the middle and skinny on the ends.

The road was a wild time, and Bear had to be careful. His lawyers warned him that it would be better for him not to go on the road. If he were busted again, bail could be revoked, and he would be remanded into the custody of the Bureau of Prisons.

Bear galumphed around the Ballroom, mumbling, "Better not to go on the road, better, better, better," his head shaking at his predicament.

Betty Cantor thought he was calling her and said, "What, Bear?"

"Better!" we greeted her when she came to the table to help roll joints, and thus she got her nickname.

Bear decided to go with the Dead. Before he left, I asked

him to put my cousin Rocky on the guest list for one of the shows. She was beautiful and self-confident, with nice tits and long blond hair. I gave her a call.

In her deep smoker's voice, she said, "Why don't you come for a visit?"

"Thanks for the invite. I'm not coming, but the Grateful Dead are playing The Image on April 19, and you're on the guest list. I want you to meet Ramrod. He's an Aries like you, and cute. It's his birthday. Bear's rooming with him."

When Bear was on the road, he often called me. He loved to talk dirty and tell me how sexy I was, but this time, I received no phone call. I tried the hotel. I did not ask the desk clerk for Owsley Stanley. No one in the band registered under their own names. I asked for "the Bear" but did not get connected. I began to worry that Bear had been busted, that the lawyers were right. In desperation, I called early in the morning and asked for Ramon Rodriques, a name Ramrod sometimes used, and I was connected.

"Where is Bear?" Grunt.

"Is he in jail?"

"No."

"Did you hook up with my cousin?

Grunt. "Call later. I'm sleeping."

When the band returned to San Francisco, in bits and pieces the story emerged. My cousin was invited back to the hotel after the gig and got very stoned. Bear seduced her. When I asked him why, he replied, "You know the best way to get to know someone, Rhoney."

The Airplane Goes Lone Eagle

The Jefferson Airplane was having a party at their Victorian mansion on Fulton Street, and more than fifty guests were attending. Bear brought LSD, DMT, sativa, hashish oil, and a thick piece of meat that he insisted Annie Corson, the Airplane's chef, cook blood rare. He would not sit down for dinner at the long table covered with a white tablecloth with the rest of us but gobbled down his steak standing up in the kitchen, talking to Annie, then left for the third floor, exclaiming, "Whoever prefers psychedelics to wine, follow me upstairs."

I loved psychedelics, but this was a banquet with connoisseur wines, and I wanted to participate. I noticed that Melissa did not follow Bear but stayed seated next to Jack at the very end of the table. Bear had handed her a dark vial.

"For anyone at the table who wants to dose," Melissa said showing off the LSD. Jack took off his South American wool jacket and hung his arm around the back of Melissa's chair.

"We should use this table for the cover of our next album," he declared bending over to look at Grace and Paul seated at opposite ends of the long table.

"Yeah," Grace spoke a bit too loud in her bawdy voice. Perhaps she had drunk too much wine, but it was after eight o'clock. "Jack, you get the fuck drunk and you can pose for the photo." Jack's luscious lips broke into a smile and he threw back his head and laughed, flaring his nostrils.

I couldn't make up my mind if I should go upstairs to be with Bear, so I stayed put without deciding, but I was not fully present. After a slow dinner that included wine tasting with every course, I went to look for him. Before I found him, I heard him. He was yelping like a dog with the pleasure of an orgasm. When he saw me, he sent the other chick away and wanted me. He was on his knees, naked and wet with sweat. We made love.

The next day at the Carousel Ballroom, I acted as if nothing had happened and checked the cables for loose connectors. The bands were hard on the equipment, and if a solder joint came undone, there would be static and noise. When Melissa arrived, we assembled all the loose cables and brought them to the shop. I had learned to solder and concentrated on the task.

Later, Janis Joplin showed up at the Carousel. She was wearing bell-bottoms and had feathers in her hair and Elvin Bishop walked behind her. She had heard what had happened at the Airplane's house and told me she felt sorry for me.

"I'm tired of Elvin," she whispered. "Take him. He's yours."

Beware the Cookie Monster

Betty Cantor followed me up to the sound booth, carrying a batch of cookies she had baked. She was famous for her chocolate chip cookies, large, crisp, and full of chocolate. She finessed the recipe on the back of the semisweet chocolate-chip morsel package by adding more baking soda.

"Yummy," I said and held out my hand for a cookie, salivating and licking my lips.

Bear was standing in front of the mixing board. He made fun of me. "Watch out, Rhoney. You'll soon look like your Russian ancestors."

Betty whispered in Bear's ear.

Man, was I jealous. What a flirt. What was she confiding to Bear? She flaunted her appeal and came on to all the guys, shaking her hips seductively, waving her blonde hair, and speaking fast in a lilting, intelligent voice. Bob Matthews and Bear were among her targets, and they were eager to teach her how to work the sound system. Bear pulled aside his leather vest, slid his hand into the inner pocket, pulled out a dark glass bottle of LSD, and gave it to Betty. She put a dose on every chocolate chip cookie.

I was outraged. I yelled, "What if some kid eats one of those?" I ran out of the Carousel. Patty Cake was sitting in her old beat-up car on Mission Street and waved to me. "Honey, baby, you look like you need a hug. Hop in. Where do you wanna go?"

"Could you drive me to Berkeley? I left a stash at the house that Bear needs," I lied.

I wasn't about to tell Patty Cake I was ready to commit suicide, how Bear's actions had devastated me. I was out of my mind.

"I'll drive you, but I gotta be back before the boys go on. I'm meeting Ramrod."

When we got to Berkeley, I pointed out the narcs parked on Sacramento near our house. She was flabbergasted. "Another reason to get out of here," I muttered. She waved to them and smiled.

I immediately darted to the bathroom and locked the door. I looked in the mirror at my face: my features faded in and out, my eyes were not next to each other, one almost on top of the other. "Owsley doesn't love you. Nobody loves you. You're not lovable." These were the words I uttered, staring at myself in the mirror. I shut my eyes. Make it go away. Stop that sound. Nobody's child with a psychotic mother. Under my skin, I saw my pulsating blood vessels, the reds and blues and purples of the veins.

Patty Cake banged on the door. "What's taking so long, Rhoney? There's no mirror in the other bathroom. I have to put on make-up."

I unfastened the latch and opened the door, and Patty Cake jumped in. She took out her makeup bag, put green eyeliner on the inner rim of her eyes and outlined her upper lids in black in the shape of the eye of Horus. Then she did the same to me. She curled my eyelashes with an eyelash curler and stroked upward with black mascara. She added rouge to my cheekbones, starting at the hairline and changing the color for the body of the cheek. We exited the bathroom, Betty Boop look-alikes: I, a slender version with long brown hair and green eyes, and Patty Cake the real McCoy, showing cleavage, wearing a short skirt and high heels, her hair in a flip. As she drove she told me a story.

"All our families are fucked up. Let me tell you what happened to Gas Girl. She comes from a wealthy family, but fucked up all the same and mean. She had an inheritance coming to her, but her parents were greedy and didn't want to give it to her. They told her she could only get her inheritance if she got married."

"Wow," I uttered, incredulous, and lowered the radio so I could hear more of her story.

"You know, Ramrod went to school with us. Larry, we called him, Lawrence Shurtliff, officially. He was so good looking with his blonde hair and sleepy blue eyes, and he never talked back to any of our teachers or parents. He was always polite. And all the parents loved him."

"Ramrod, the angel."

"And he's easy to talk to because he doesn't say much, so Gas Girl laid it all out for him, how she had to be married to get her inheritance."

"Wow," I commented. "Ramrod hates meanness."

"Gas Girl's parents were awful to her, but like the rest of our parents, they were taken with Ramrod. Gas Girl told Ramrod, "You're the type that every mother wants her daughter to marry. What if you married me? That would show my parents. I'll buy you a motorcycle with my inheritance money.' Ramrod thought about it for about a half a second, and immediately they went to City Hall and got married. Gas Girl got her inheritance, and Ramrod got his motorcycle."

Patty Cake rubbed her belly and her eyes were starry.

"Are you fucking Ramrod?" I asked.

She turned to me and nodded yes.

"I want to get pregnant," she confided.

I do too, I thought, but would Bear want a child with me?

Tuesday Night Jam poster art

© Stanley Mouse

Lighting Up the Dark Night

I wandered around the Carousel Ballroom with nothing to do. Patty Cake and Betty were slouched at the counter at the grill like working girls on a slow night. Betty's long blonde hair was tied back in a ponytail. With her bell-bottom jeans and big butt, she looked like a sexy Valley Girl. Patty Cake was wearing a miniskirt, and her tight top pushed out her big boobs. They were bored.

Bear was on the road with the Grateful Dead, the Jefferson Airplane, and Quicksilver, and the Carousel was dark. No outside light got in, and the house lights were dimmed, barely reflected on the polished wooden dance floor. Rakow constantly complained about money and bitched at me that Bear was not supporting the Carousel. I didn't get what he was talking about. We had filled the hall with the best of blues—Chuck Barry and John Lee Hooker, Santana, and Erma Franklin. Along with the main act, we booked local psychedelic rock bands like It's A Beautiful Day, Moby Grape, Frumious Bandersnatch, and Initial Shock. The Carousel was rocking. I wondered what was ailing him. It was only May.

Elvin Bishop walked into the Carousel carrying his guitar case and grabbed me in a firm embrace.

"Here I am," he stated. "Janis sent me."

"Yes, Pigboy." I squirmed out of his arms and headed for the stage. "You wanna plug into Bear's system, right? Follow me."

Bear had set up the system so all I had to do was turn on the power. I gave Elvin a cable and plugged the other end into an amplifier. Elvin adjusted the mic stand. I headed out front to hear him better. Rakow came out of the office, and Jonathan Reister and everyone else who was around listened as Elvin played. We all went gaga. He played Chicago blues with a sentimental Oklahoma twang. He played for twenty minutes and we all applauded.

"Elvin, you are fabulous." I touched his overalls and his soft curly hair.

"Any time you want to come to the Carousel, Bear's system is here for you."

Of course, Elvin took me up on my offer, and while the Grateful Dead were on the road he became a regular at the Carousel, practicing the guitar, singing the blues in a gentle voice, and acting rowdy. If only Elvin had a backup band. I imagined the sound, and then I thought, why couldn't the Carousel invite individual musicians to play together when we had no shows scheduled? Bear's PA system was available. Wasn't his credo "nobody owns anything, and stuff is just here for use"? I figured, we may as well keep the Carousel open for business, get the kids off the street, and give musicians the opportunity to practice on the best sound system available at the time.

Garcia walked into the Carousel late afternoon while Elvin was on stage playing the guitar, and we stood together and listened. Garcia was very particular about guitar players. He didn't care how fast someone played or how many notes they could fit into a bar. He was after tone and originality.

Elvin bowed to our applause.

I told Garcia my brainstorm.

He said, "Great idea, Rhoney. Let's talk to Rakow."

We found him in his office. I laid out my plan. "We

invite musicians—a guitarist, a bass player, a drummer—
to use Bear's sound system and play together. We tell them
it's not for pay, it's a chance to use the sound system and
play with other musicians. There'll be no contractual
issues, no additional costs. Everyone wants to jam with
you," I said to Garcia.

He laughed. "Any time we're not on the road, I'll be here.
You'll have no problem getting together a band, Rhoney."

"We'll open the Carousel once a week for a musician's jam,
at no charge."

"No," said Rakow, "we charge for tickets."

Garcia decided. "We charge a dollar!"

Rakow wasn't about to contradict Garcia.

"We can charge for food," Rakow concluded, as always
interested in the money.

"You'll need a poster and handbills to promote it,"
Garcia declared confidentially.

"Wait a minute," interrupted Rakow, "that's expensive."

"We can print one poster advertising the jam, not the
bands, and use it every week," I suggested.

Garcia liked that. "Go see Mouse, Rhoney. He'll do it."

Elvin Bishop, wearing his usual straw hat and overalls,
met me in front of Mouse's studio, an old one-room
firehouse in a nonresidential area of San Francisco.

"You look like a farmer," I said.

He grinned at me and pulled out a polka-dotted bow
tie and clipped it on.

"Now you look like a goofball farmer."

We knocked on the door and entered an almost-square
room with very high ceilings and brick walls. Mouse
expected me.

"This is my friend Elvin Bishop. He's been playing
guitar with Bear's equipment."

"How's Bear?" he asked solicitously, peering at me through his wire-rimmed glasses. He played with his mustache.

"Bear's great. He's on the road. Garcia told me to talk to you. We need a poster to advertise this new thing we're doing at the Carousel we're calling the Tuesday Night Jam," I explained. "Musicians get together and play off Bear's sound system."

Mouse sat behind his drawing table and began drawing with a pencil on an open sketch pad, staring at Elvin as if he were the model.

Elvin, leaning against a drawing board, drawled, "Why don't you let Pig Boy be your poster boy?"

"We have to advertise the jam, not one musician." I got right into his face. "The jam, like a jam jar."

Mouse bent over in laughter.

Elvin jumped up. "That's it. A pig, not a Pig Boy!"

"Wow!" I exclaimed. "Pigging out with a jam jar!"

Mouse never looked up from his drawing board.

Elvin pursed his lips together like a snout and snorted and stretched. I laughed.

"How about lots of pigs?"

"One pig around a jam jar is enough," Mouse advised.

As it was practical, I agreed. "We want room for information."

"What do you want it to read?" asked Mouse.

"Tuesday Night Jam, Carousel Ballroom, One Dollar." Then I added, "Deep, rich colors, please."

"The tone of the colors depends a lot on the printer. I use Tea Lautrec. He's the best in San Francisco. He lets the artist have control. We work together to get the right ink mixture and color combinations. Sometimes we mix the inks on the spot to get the right colors. Guesswork!"

"Wow! How many should we print?"

"Talk to Tea Lautrec. Once I've done the artwork and have a paste-up, we'll meet there."

"Okay," I said. "Mid-May is the first Tuesday Night Jam."

Tea Lautrec, whose real name was Levon Mosgofian, looked more like a bohemian Parisian than a hippie. His photo-offset lithographic printing shop was located in the commercial district of San Francisco, near Howard and Mission. The shop was small, a bare room with a wooden floor and a cage for the printing press. He proudly showed us the large press and explained why it was called a one-color, sheet-feed press. Individual sheets of paper were pulled through the press one at a time and run through several times for multiple colors. He showed me a poster with no color that looked like a negative.

"How weird. It's like an absence of color. I love it."

"You love it because it's different. Take it," he said. "You can have any posters you want."

"Wow," I replied. "You are so generous."

Elvin and I walked around the shop, looking through posters like records in a record shop. There was a poster of a guy with flowers in his head instead of brains. There were posters with photographs: Jim Morrison scowling, The Charlatans showing off their cowboy saloon finery, James Joyce looking like a literary giant. I saw a poster advertising Jean-Luc Goddard's movie "Weekend" with a fantastic car crash.

Mouse arrived with the artwork, and Tea and he set to work. The paste-up, or mechanical, was a series of acetate overlays that separated the design according to the different colors for printing. Tea took photographic images and prepared the aluminum printing plates with chemicals to make the image areas receptive to the ink.

Mouse was looking through a standard color book to select the inks.

Tea said, "If you don't see the color you want, we can mix."

"It's a crapshoot," declared Mouse, after combining inks on the paper and studying the colors until he finally approved. Then the printing began.

"I suggest that when we print the poster, we also print handbills, the same image but smaller. These are good for advertising and not expensive," Tea advised.

"We can staple the bills to telephone poles and lampposts," Elvin added.

"How many posters do you want? We do lots of five hundred or a thousand."

"Five hundred is all we need," I replied.

"We're printing two posters on one sheet and four handbills on another. That way you save money."

I watched Tea carefully adjust the paper feeder. He said to run 1,000 sheets through the press took approximately fifteen minutes and used about a pound of ink, and 500 sheets wasn't that much different. Drying between plates was forty-five minutes, and during that time the press was cleaned, the new plate attached, and fresh ink added.

Mouse spoke to Tea. "You can do the rest without me. I trust you."

"I know what you want. I'll come up with the color combinations," Tea reassured Mouse. Tea suggested that we come back the next day, as the ink required twelve hours to fully dry.

In the morning they were ready.

"The blue is so electric," I commented. "Mouse said you were the best."

"Phthalocyanine blue," he replied.

I thanked him and kissed him goodbye. Elvin and I carried rolls of posters and handbills out to Bear's car and loaded them into the backseat.

"Do you think it matters that we didn't put on the date? I know we decided, but maybe that was the wrong decision. How will anyone know when to come?"

"Hippies know," Mouse said. "They have antennae for rock 'n' roll."

I took out my Murine bottle and put a drop under Elvin's tongue before dosing myself. We put a poster on every goddamn telephone pole in San Francisco.

The Monday before the Tuesday Night Jam I was in a panic. I was convinced no one would come.

"So what?" Garcia said. "We'll play to you."

Bear was running the sound, and I asked him to promise me that he would not be late for the gig, but he said, "I don't know, Rhoney. I have a lot to do." The stage was set up, the PA on—all the musicians had to do was plug in, but I wanted to record the show, and for that I needed Bear.

Tuesday, May 21, 1968, standing on the side of the stage, looking out at an almost full house, I felt proud.

Garcia said, "Rhoney, come on stage and introduce us."

I stumbled into the light on stage and grabbed Garcia to steady myself. I was afraid to open my mouth.

"The Tuesday Night Jam," I began. There was so much audience noise that nothing else could be heard. I danced to the back of the stage as the jam band roared to life. Victory.

Carousel Bell Tolls

Disaster. We were losing money at the Carousel. Bear had bankrolled the Grateful Dead for years with his profits from LSD, but he refused to support the Carousel. He needed the money for his defense, and he believed the Carousel should be self-supporting.

The Grateful Dead were making more money than ever, the Jefferson Airplane were the highest paid American rock'n'roll band, and Quicksilver was in demand all over the country. Our house bands weren't going to bail us out. The lease agreement Ron Rakow had signed with the landlord, Bill Fuller, required a monthly payment that we could meet only if we exceeded the capacity of the Carousel, and the fire marshals showed up every weekend to make sure we had not sold more tickets than the specified capacity. The magical era of the Carousel Ballroom had lasted six months, but now it was at a dead end.

Rakow went crazy. When the fire commissioner locked the doors on June 19, Rakow refused to leave. Suddenly, he broke out of the building like a cowboy at a holdup, smashing a window and climbing down a fire escape onto Market Street. A lot of good that did. First he was locked in; then he was locked out. Miraculously, the commissioner unlocked the doors, and the next day we held a meeting.

Ken Kesey came down from Oregon to preside over another discussion.

"What should we put on the marquee?" he asked.

One of the chicks said, "Fare Thee Well."

Kesey commented, "Not bad."

"We want a philosophical message," I said, "that teaches something."

Then Kesey pulled out a copy of the I Ching, the Book of Changes, read to himself, and finally said with his finger in the air, "Everything changes; nothing lasts."

At the closing of the Carousel Ballroom, the last week in June, 1968, the marquee read "Nothing Lasts." Janis and Big Brother played June 22 and 23, Saturday and Sunday nights. The mood was somber but the music soared. Janis sang "Piece of My Heart" for her final performance as if she were singing for her life, and Bear recorded.

Within days, Bill Graham negotiated a better deal on the lease directly with the landlord in Ireland and reopened the Carousel as the Fillmore West with Big Brother and Janis Joplin. We felt burned. The Grateful Dead would not play the Fillmore West for several weeks. None of us would even attend shows there until Bill Graham booked Ornette Coleman, August 5. That got Garcia to go. He was a jazz aficionado.

After that, the ice was broken. Bill Graham offered the Grateful Dead five nights in a two-week period at the new Fillmore West, August 20, 21, 22, 30, and 31. They were preparing to go into the studio to record *Aoxomoxoa* and wanted the practice in front of a large audience. To seduce the band even more, Bill Graham said that Bear could leave his equipment set up at the Carousel. Bear was still depressed.

"Our neighbors on Valley Street are too close. I want to move."

I looked at him sideways. "Does that mean you want to move to Marin?"

Mountain Girl told me that she and Jerry were looking in Larkspur, and Hunter intended to live with them. Everyone was moving to Marin.

"Noooo!" Bear stretched out the negative and it filled our house. He said, "Look for a house in Berkeley."

I looked at listings from the local newspaper and found another house designed by the Fox brothers, the same architects who built the Valley Street house, on the north side of Berkeley. Bear did not like the location.

I said, "What's the matter with the location? It's close to Timothy Leary's house."

"That's exactly the point."

"But Bear, you visit Leary."

"Don't you notice how quickly I leave? I cannot abide his lust for publicity. He is a magnet for attention. Look for another house."

He rejected every house I showed him.

Mountain Girl called again to say they had found a house on the edge of Madrone Canyon, and Janis was living on the same street.

"I want to move to Marin. Don't I count? Isn't what I want important?"

"You don't have to move with me, Rhoney. You can do what you want."

Indian music gave me clarity, so I drove up to the Ali Akbar Khan School of Music, situated in a beautiful Spanish-style multilevel house with arts-and-crafts detailing in the secluded hills of Oakland, southeast of Berkeley. While I was listening to a morning raga played by Khansahib with Vince Delgado on tabla, it occurred to me that this place would be perfect for Bear. With all the rooms and levels, he could live here with any number of Grateful Dead family. Ramrod had already agreed to live with Bear when he moved.

I called Bear, and he met me at the Indian music school. "This place has such good vibes," I said. "They're moving out at the end of the month."

He laughed. "That might be some good news. Could we get a lease? This is just up the hill from the Claremont Hotel."

We walked around the house where there was a swimming pool and a separate entrance in the back. Stately trees reached beyond the third floor. We went back inside which was atop a long stairway from the front door.

"Look, Bear, I can stand at the top of the stairs and see who's coming."

"Yes, but you can't see the front door from any of the windows."

The kitchen was large and round, with ample room for a table and guitars. There were several bedrooms, a very large living room, a hallway, and two bathrooms upstairs. If only Bear would say "perfect!"

He said, "This is it. I knew I would find it. I don't like not seeing the front door, but I want the lease. Can you get it?"

Vince Delgado, administrative head of the Ali Akbar Khan school, was dying to perform percussion with the Grateful Dead, and the band would be playing at the Berkeley Community Center on my birthday. What if we invited Ali Akbar Khan and his students to open for the Dead? If Vince could realize his dream, he would turn over the lease to Bear. Nobody else would get a shot at the house.

"I'll pay cash. I'll pay a full year in advance," declared Bear.

I had a trade. Teasing, I swayed my hips.

"Let's make a deal," I said, imagining exquisite music in my head. "You get the Indian musicians a gig with the Grateful Dead, and I'll get you the lease."

At the end of summer of 1968, when the Indian musicians moved out of the house in Oakland Hills, Bear moved in. Betty and Bob Mathews took the downstairs apartment, and Ramrod moved into the bedroom next to Bear's. Weir camped out in the living room. Bear did not invite me to move to Oakland Hills. He said, "You can stay at Valley Street. I still have time on the lease."

My mother always said, "You'll never have a man of your own." Maybe she was right.

September 20, 1968, at the Berkeley Community Theater in Berkeley, California, on a Friday night, Bear and I set up the stage. We brought in an Oriental rug and our home speakers. We covered the Dead's large Fender amplifiers at the back of the stage with Indian bedspreads. Bear crept along the stage, head bent, placing the new Sennheiser microphones. Particularly for the drums, he kept the microphones low. Sometimes Bear got it exactly right, and this was one of those times.

The Indian musicians opened with a raga performed by Ali Akbar Khan on sarod. The Grateful Dead performed "Alligator," conceived under the influence of LSD, written tribally, with contributions from all the band members, including Pigpen. Vince Delgado, dark eyes shining, sat in on percussion. For my birthday Bear had bought me a tanpura, a drone instrument with four strings. All I had to do was strum one string at a time and keep the rhythm. That was easy. Staying focused was harder. I was seduced by any distraction.

Zen Center

Living alone in the house in Berkeley, I realized I had no direction. Owsley did not need me; my place with the Grateful Dead was uncertain, and I needed to feel useful. Whenever a challenge arose, Bear would say, "Take LSD," and I'd take a dose, but I also took meditation.

It was very quiet when I entered the Zen temple on Bush Street in San Francisco. *Zazen* had already started, and the meditators were in their cubicles. At the very top of the Zen temple, I sat down on a black cushion in a meditation pose and faced the blank wall, barely sweating from my climb. I recited my mantra from Maharishi.

"Sheom, sheom," I said, concentrating on my breathing. I kept my eyes half open. "Sheom . . . sheom . . ."

I felt a stick strike my shoulder. My first impulse was to flail around in confrontation, but I was curious and slowly turned around. Roshi Suzuki was standing over me in his long black robes beating me on a shoulder with a stick. His bald head gleamed, and he was smiling, laughing as he struck me again.

"Blow of compassion," he said. "Direct teaching."

The gongs sounded the end of the service, and I floated down the steps and out to my car. I headed for Bear's house in the Oakland Hills as if everything were the same. On the Bay Bridge, suddenly I became one with the road, with the car, the steering wheel, and my propulsion through space to a destination was natural and effortless. This had never happened to me before. I felt as if I were part of Divinity yet in this world—the nirvana of legend.

When I got to Bear's, Bobby Weir was the only one there. He was sitting on the couch, practicing his guitar. His head was close to the body of the guitar, and he was listening hard to every note he played, so absorbed in the sound that I did not want to disturb him, but he looked up when I entered the room. I asked him how he was doing.

"Mighty fine," he said.

"Well, I'm not. I was at the San Francisco Zen Center." I told him what happened to me on the Bay Bridge. "I melted into my environment. What was outside was inside. We were all one. It's a miracle that I didn't have an accident."

Bobby was not surprised. He was on a macrobiotic diet and into everything Japanese, and he understood.

"I got high naturally, Bobby. I didn't need hallucinogens." I couldn't stop reliving my experience.

He said, "That's what I've been saying. We've always known what we've seen on LSD, we can see on the natch . . . mighty weird."

Bobby was very skinny, muscle and bones, and he looked young and impressionable, but he was unwavering in his rejection of LSD. He felt he had taken LSD enough to realize the nature of "high," and he wanted to do it naturally.

"It'll all fall together. It'll come into focus for you," he said.

"I didn't even have a sense of self."

Bobby nodded, humble and thoughtful. "You were transported somewhere else. The grace and elegance just come through if you get out of the way and let it happen."

Revolver was on the stereo: "Turn off your mind. . . . It is not dying. . . . It is being . . . Love is all and love is everyone."

When Bear got home, I told him my experience. "Zen meditation got me so high that I lost all sense of boundaries, but I was perfectly safe."

"So what?" he said. "LSD does that to you."

"Bear," I said. "The point is, this was natural. I didn't take LSD. I didn't take anything. I got high while I was driving. I left my body while I was in the car, on the Bay Bridge, coming to see you from the Zen Center."

"I don't get your point."

"Can we go see Alan Watts? Maybe I can talk to him." I couldn't explain it to Bear, and I couldn't solve my dilemma by taking more LSD.

Alan Watts was a scholar of Zen Buddhism and in 1964 had written a book, *The Way of Zen*. I called and got an appointment immediately. Hisayo, my friend from Indian music school, was his secretary.

Alan lived in a community of houseboats in the Sausalito harbor. It was a long walk down the docks to his boat. The houseboat was so spacious that I almost forgot I was on a boat. Bear and I sat on a sofa facing Alan on his chair across an old glass-topped table that contained a shell collection. I told Alan everything about my experience.

"You had an experience of *kensho*, seeing into your own nature." Alan continued. "Some people get there from psychedelics, some from meditation, some from study, some from lineage."

Bear jumped in. "LSD was the engine that drove your experience of enlightenment."

"Bear thinks LSD gave me the experience. As long as it's positive, it's thanks to LSD."

We headed for the kitchen. I took the bar stool. Alan put on an apron and heated a cast-iron pan on top of the stove.

"Look, Bear, Alan cooks meat the same way you do!"

Alan served the steaks on wooden plates.

"This is incredible," I said. "Owsley has wooden plates for meat, too."

I stood up to eat and I ate fast. Alan never stopped talking. He was chattier than Owsley. "Can you tell me more about your experience?"

"It was the loss of self-identity that was so profound, that one aspect of myself could drive the car but what felt like my real self had merged with the universe. Isn't it amazing?"

Alan chuckled and spoke quietly. "You have experienced nonduality. The rational view of reality is dualistic—subject and object. In Western society, the dualistic perception is so strong that any other view has remained unquestioned until now. We are pioneers in more than psychedelics. For centuries, sages have contemplated and studied nondualism, or *advaita*, which literally means 'not two.' This view is the basis of the Upanishads of ancient India, and Krishna's teaching to Arjuna in the Bhagavad Gita, and the Vedanta teachings—the utter absence of any differentiation between Atman (the Self) and Brahman."

"If 'Brahman' means 'god,' I have to tell you, I'm not into this god stuff."

Alan laughed. "Think of it as experiencing the divine nature. Buddhism is the least god-centered of all religions."

"I have a mantra from TM. Shall I practice? I'm supposed to repeat the mantra silently for twenty minutes twice a day."

"Excellent. Chant and breathe."

Bear repeated his mantra: "LSD is the easiest way to reach enlightenment. Religion isn't pure enough. There's always bullshit a foot deep."

My inner voice said, "That's what I used to think," as I let Bear put a drop under my tongue.

Debauchee Rides with Goldfinger

Everybody could see I was depressed when I wasn't with Bear. But they couldn't see inside me, where I was hysterical and headed for one of my self-destructive spirals. I had an affair. What better way to get to know somebody? I started smoking opium because it fit the role and made the sex impersonal.

I spent a weekend at a notorious resort in the wooded valley of California, adjacent to the wine country. It was supposedly developed by the Mafia in the 1940s. The hot springs were world famous, enjoyed by rich hippies. Everyone was stoned, beautiful, and naked, soaking in a succession of hot tubs. When a storm hit, I ducked into an old shed filled with a herd of psychedelic, wet hippies. I spotted somebody I knew—Goldfinger, a swashbuckling San Francisco drug dealer who had lost his hand in a propeller of a private airplane loaded with drugs in South America. Bear had gifted him with a jewel-studded prosthesis with a hook.

"Where's Bear?" he asked, surprised to see me.

"Not here," I told him.

A wet, mud-covered chick rushed into the wooden shed. "The cops are coming up the road! Anyone who has dope do something about it now!"

Goldfinger grabbed me. "Let's go." His new 911 Porsche was waiting under a redwood tree.

"Fasten your seat belt," he commanded. "We'll flatten out this mountain road and leave the cops in the mud."

The rain pounded the windshield, and I could barely see out, but Goldfinger thundered down the muddy road, shifting the Porsche and occasionally resting his claw on my knee to comfort me. At a bend in the road, the cops passed in the other direction, and we roared right by them, Goldfinger pushing the elegant machine to its limit.

When we got to San Francisco, we went to Finnochio's at 508 Broadway. Men performed dressed as show-biz women. "Would you cut my steak?" Goldfinger kindly asked.

The next day I told Owsley, thinking he would be pleased with my getaway, but he was furious. "How dare you go off with Goldfinger? What if you had been caught with him? He is the most wanted drug dealer in California."

Owsley was the most wanted.

Nothing was working for me, not the music scene, not the Grateful Dead, not LSD, certainly not Owsley. I was unemployed in my early twenties and without a profession. Enough, I said to myself, become a teacher. Didn't my father tell me to become a teacher? "It's that or typing," he'd say.

In California, the requirement for a credential in teaching was completion of one year of graduate school in education. I went to Sproul Hall at UC Berkeley and picked up an application for graduate school admission in the Department of Education. The campus was bustling with students returning for classes. I loved all the action and the intellectual energy of the environment. School I could do!

I got a call from a friend who had a meth lab. He was living in Black Point, the last outpost in Marin before Solano County, California, at the mouth of the Sacramento River. His house was high on the hill overlooking the mud flats, ten minutes from downtown Novato, but so remote that the roads were not paved and the grade was steep. Little hills with hairpin turns helped you lose your way.

He had a nasal voice and he spoke like a robot. "The house down in the flats is getting fixed up. I spoke to the owner. He wants to rent it next spring. Cute little place. Nothing there but an inlet off the Sacramento River. Thought you might be interested."

"Wow," I said, "I want to see it."

As soon as I saw the house, I fell in love. The owner lived in Sacramento; the closest neighbor was a goat farm, and the backyard was a tributary of the Sacramento River where egrets nested in the mudflats. The road to the house was unpaved. That could be an advantage. I could hear who was coming before they got there.

Frankie Hanky-Panky Takes Me to Kesey's

I drove directly to San Francisco, to the Fillmore (our old Carousel) where Bear was packing up equipment for the road. The Grateful Dead were going to the East Coast for a three-week tour. They would be gone for Thanksgiving. I stepped out of the sunny day through the dark stage door. Equipment filled the stage and floor. There was no way to walk a clear path to get to Bear, but I struggled through the mass of cables and spooled coils, preamps with tubes popping out of sockets.

I interrupted Bear as he was talking to Ramrod. "I found a house in Marin. I want to move."

"We've had this discussion before."

"It's a great deal."

"You know my decision." When Bear had determined his opinion, there was no changing his mind, but I was strong too. I pumped up my ribs and started to say, "I respect you, but—" when Bear spoke. He put his hands on my shoulders to emphasize what he was going to say, and I tripped on a piece of equipment, lost my footing, and fell hard on my left wrist.

I screamed in pain and anger, "Fuck you, Bear. You don't care about me. You don't listen to me. I am miserable in Berkeley and want to move." I didn't care who else heard me, I was so mad. But when I saw Frankie holding hands with Mickey on the side of the stage, I was embarrassed. She was a Rockette or a go-go dancer or the girl wanted by the Shindog on Hullabaloo, and she looked like Jacqueline Kennedy. She took me aside.

"I saw Bear push you."

"Frankie, I fell."

"Time to get out of Dodge. I'm having trouble with Mickey. Let's go to Kesey's for Thanksgiving." She had this no-nonsense way of talking. She gently touched my swelling wrist.

"We better get you to a doctor."

We went to a doctor's office in San Francisco. He put a cast on my arm up to my elbow. A day before Thanksgiving, we left for Oregon.

A bus trip was something I had never done. In my family, buses were lower class. But this was an adventure, and a chance to bond with Frankie, the sexiest chick in our scene. Nobody was certain of her story and she let the mystery fly.

Frankie confided in me that she was leaving Mickey and going to London to work for George Harrison.

"Oh, Frankie, my favorite Beatle!"

"Kesey may like the idea."

When we arrived at the farm, it was night and Kesey and the Merry Pranksters who lived with him were going to the local school gym to play volleyball.

"Let's go," said Frankie.

"But I don't know how to play volleyball."

"You'll learn."

"I have a cast on my arm."

"Use your other arm. You're right-handed."

I realized, if I'm with Frankie, I can do anything.

I followed her, observing her closely, watching her jump up lightly, lobbing the ball to a teammate. She landed on the balls of her feet. Frankie was a natural, gracefully returning a serve. Even rubbing her sweaty hands on her white skirt she was elegant. I joined in and imitated her, and before too long I was part of the team. I wondered, how do you keep your identity when it is so easy to merge?

When we got back to Kesey's, I asked, "Where's the bathroom?" Kesey gestured with his head and pointed. He was laid back on the couch, Frankie sitting next to him. "But there's no door!" I exclaimed.

Frankie laughed, "What do you care, Rhoney? You're a hippie." I wandered around the house, looking for a bathroom with a door, but every bathroom I found had no door. The carpeting went into the bathroom, as if the bathroom were just another part of the house. I had no choice but to forgo privacy. I sat on the toilet and listened to Kesey and Frankie chatting away, planning an escapade in London, as the rain beat down outside the window on the farm.

"What will we do for money?" Kesey asked.

"We'll use other people's money. Someone rich will come along." Frankie took a deep puff off her brown cigarette.

"Let's be there before Christmas."

"Beatlemania for Christmas."

Leroy came in. He was living in a trailer at Kesey's place, behind the main house. He had moved out of his converted church in San Francisco and given up the hustle of drug dealing for a simpler life, which he had found here in the woods. He was paying me a lot of attention and staring me straight in the eye when he talked. He was light-skinned and liked white chicks. "At Kesey's," he told me, "everyone is welcome. Kesey finds a role for you."

Frankie whispered, "He is so cool. Why don't you spend the night with him?"

He was Bear's dealer and I knew his woman, but he wanted me and there were only so many beds. Nature took its course.

Later, Kesey complimented me. He told me I had an amazing ability to adapt. I fit right in with these Oregon hokies and he could tell I had never been in this type of environment before. I understood his praise, but it also sounded as if I had no core or that I was chameleon-like. That's not complimentary.

"You are a trickster, illusory. Even your name is a prankster name."

"I don't feel it."

"Wear one color sock on one foot and a different color sock on the other foot."

I laughed heartily and immediately found a different-colored sock.

On the bus back to San Francisco, Frankie told me that Kesey had named her Frankie Hanky-Panky. He would go with her to London.

"What will you do?"

"I'm a dancer, honey. I can do anything."

The bus swayed and Frankie's lithe body moved rhythmically, as if she were fluid.

"Why don't you come with us? You need to get away from this scene."

"No," I said. "Bear needs me. He knows that."

Sitting next to Frankie on the bus, passing through farmland and countryside, I imagined my path. I saw myself as an Earth Mother with a child. "I don't have to live with him," I said more to myself than to her, but she put her hand to her chin and thought about it.

"Why are we so dependent on men?"

An answer stammered from my lips. "Well—they depend on us too."

"No way like us," said Frankie. "Bear thinks he left you, and Mickey does not get that I left him."

I looked out at the Mexicans working in a giant field of row after row of some plant I could not identify. It had been a year since the bust, and I was still living alone at Valley Street. The Feds continued to watch; they were fighting a war against boredom and they were losing. Melissa rarely came to Berkeley, so I visited her in San Francisco. Jack claimed that her red Citroen sports car made her too easy to follow. Jack blamed Bear for this burden. As if.

One day I was walking down Sacramento Street and a plainclothesman sitting in his parked car said, "Hi, Melissa." They were still mixing us up. Later, when I told Jack, he was surprised. He said, "I don't see it."

Alembics

In a family meeting at Mickey Hart's barn in Novato, Mickey's father, Lenny Hart, a former drummer during the big band era, proposed to be the manager of the Grateful Dead. He stood up in his plaid shirt, tight jeans, and cowboy boots, and he spoke as if from the heart. He promised he was the right man for the job. We did not know what to decide. No one wanted a manager telling us what to do. Most of us came from dysfunctional families who thought we were wacky or drug addicts. At least Lenny Hart acted like he believed in us. Maybe we could define old roles in new ways—everyone with an equal voice.

When Lenny finished we applauded, but after he left, we discussed the meeting. Bear was suspicious. Mickey told us that his father had given up Judaism to become a born again Christian. Oy vey.

"Well that was weird," I whispered to Bear.

"Wasn't being Jewish enough for him?" Bear asked.

"Like Dylan," I responded.

Mickey was talking. "He's a reverend now."

"The Reverend Lenny Hart," Garcia said, smiling and shaking his black shaggy hair.

Bear didn't buy it. He didn't go for his manner. Garcia said, "Why not give him a shot?" He doubted Lenny could be worse than what we already had.

We made a decision: Lenny Hart would be manager, and Melissa and I would be secretaries. As it was, Melissa spent so much time with Jack that most of the job would fall to me.

☙

The Grateful Dead rented a warehouse in Marin, a big empty place close to Highway 101, next to Hamilton Air Force Base. Loud rock 'n' roll could not disturb the military planes taking off and landing day and night—and we never complained.

The warehouse was divided into a bare, unheated concrete rehearsal space, a reception area with a bathroom, and a long back area with living quarters upstairs. Out front was a large asphalt parking lot where anyone entering or leaving was visible. Bear approved and moved in all his equipment. He bought space heaters for the rehearsal hall. They looked like animal cages in a science laboratory, and someone was always tripping over them, but Bear assured us they were "the latest in technology for safety, efficiency, and noise reduction."

Bear and Ramrod pushed the amps into different positions, chasing the sound, their ears bent to the speakers.

"The sound sucks, but what can you expect in an empty concrete warehouse?"

Bear agreed, "We need to work on it."

I thought, maybe I can have a role.

When the furniture arrived from former Grateful Dead locations—two desks, odd chairs, and a faded velvet couch—we distributed it as evenly as we could in the front rooms. The couch went into the sitting room next to the dinky bathroom, which smelled of urine no matter how much we cleaned. Guys. The two desks went one behind the other. We got phone service. Melissa and I mainly sat on the desks with our legs crossed, as if we were in a secretary commercial. There was no kitchen, so we ended up snacking and getting fat, eating junk food—potato chips, pretzels, what Mickey Hart called "glups." Mickey was never fat.

The Grateful Dead spent most of their time at the warehouse. Weir said there was no point in finding a place to live as he was either on the road or at the warehouse. He commandeered the sitting room next to the office as his bedroom and used the velvet couch as his bed.

"Feels like 710," he said, sardonically, recalling the place the Grateful Dead had lived in The Haight.

At the far end of the warehouse, Bear set up shop and went to work on the sound. He was a pack rat and saved everything—duplicates, triplicates, quadruplicates. In his endless quest for better-quality sound, he had amassed an arsenal of equipment and needed quippies to schlep it. In the name of psychedelic alchemy, he deemed the warehouse "Alembic."

"The receiving vessel is the alembic. Alembic: the distillation vessel used in the alchemical reaction," Bear said, pontificating, and the band listened. They were good listeners.

Bob Thomas painted a logo of a hand holding a mystical "A" in a myriad of colors. We were the many fingers of the cosmic hand, multicolored, biblical in scope, psychedelic. We would generate pure transformation like the alchemical transmutation of lead into gold. Rich.

With space to implement his ideas, Bear moved ahead on his plans to capture the magic of a Grateful Dead concert in a live recording. He took enough acid to slay a dragon and determined he needed expertise that he couldn't find in books or the existing technology. Then he

met Ron Wickersham at Pacific Recording Studio where
the Dead were still recording *Aoxomoxoa*, and he felt he had
found his man. He invited Ron to move to Alembic to build
a system for live recording. Ron designed a mic-splitter box
to feed the mics from the stage into channels of the tape
board. The Grateful Dead leased an Ampex sixteen-track,
and the quippies hauled it to shows at the Avalon and the
Fillmore. The result was *Live/Dead*, which was recorded in
January, February, and March of 1969 but was not released
until November. Bob Thomas worked on the artwork at
Alembic, doing a wash of a psychedelic princess on paper.
He progressed to acrylics and canvas, mixing paints and
muddying the colors for the figures of girls, and using pure
color for the back cover depicting Americana. Ramrod said
he wanted to buy the paintings, and I said I wanted to buy
them, so we split them between us. Everyone was invited
to take photos of the band and the family to be used in the
album. We wanted this album to represent a family effort.

Often I stayed at Bear's house in the Oakland Hills.
When I arrived, he was on the telephone. Yakety-yak.

"Frankie's on the phone from London." Bear handed the
receiver to me.

"Hi, girlfriend," Frankie said. "I'm coming home, and I
want you to pick me up at the airport!" Her voice was soft
and raspy, a young girl's voice, like a cultured debutante.

When I met Frankie at the airport, I wore velvet tie-
dyed bell-bottoms, cowboy boots, and a low-cut gauzy top
with long sleeves. I wrapped strings of beads around my
wrists as bracelets. In my hair, I pinned a wolf's tail.

Her short curly hair was messed up from the long
flight, and she was dressed casually in tights and a white
T-shirt, a cigarette dangling from her graceful fingers. It
was 1969.

"Frankie," I shouted and ran to her. Her eyelashes were long and thick with mascara, and she had a heavenly scent, like Southern magnolias.

On the drive, I spouted the latest about our scene.

"Everyone's moved to Marin except Bear and me, of course. Tell me about you. Did you meet the Beatles?"

"I'm one of the girls singing backup on their latest studio recording."

"What studio recording? What song?"

She wouldn't tell me. She refused to tell anybody. If she did sing in the background during the time she was in London, I'm hoping that it was "Hey, Jude."

"What happened with George Harrison?"

"It's complicated, but I'll tell you . . . George Harrison is a true gentleman."

"So what does that mean?"

Frankie smiled and lit a cigarette. "Jimi Hendrix is the biggest thing in rock 'n' roll, and they all know it." Frankie spoke breathlessly. "With Pennebaker's film of Monterey Pop in wide release, Jimi's top of the pops."

We went to Bear's in the East Bay. We were alone and I put on one of Bear's rehearsal tapes of the Grateful Dead. We settled down on the thick Turkish rugs in the living room.

I sang from my chest as if I were an old mammy, "Lay down my sweet . . ."

Frankie interrupted, "Shh, honey, I want to hear the boys sing."

She listened, her face intent.

"I hear Weir's voice." Frankie uncrossed her legs and got up. "I'm going out for a cigarette."

We went downstairs and stood by the swimming pool. The Sequoias shaded the sky. I took a long puff off Frankie's cigarette.

"What's been happening with you and Bear and Melissa?"
I filled her in with the latest.

Frankie's angular jaw was set in a strong pose. "She's with Jack Casady, and she still comes around Bear! Oh, you poor baby. I could never take that. I'm the sugar, baby. I could never share a man. I need too much attention. Leave Bear."

I knew Frankie was right, but she is a Leo and I am a Virgo, and Virgos are loyal to a fault.

"Why don't you fuck Hunter and see what happens?"

That threw me. She kept talking.

"When Christie's in England, you could step in. Just leave Hunter some breathing space. He needs that."

"Frankie!" I acted horrified.

"What?" She always spoke her mind. I loved her for it.

The tall Sequoias stretched their shadows into the pool. The air was crisp and clear. Frankie moved her long neck.

"Does anyone use the swimming pool?"

"No. It's not heated." She stripped off her clothes and dived into the deep end. I followed.

When we got inside Frankie asked, "Where's the tequila?"

Bear didn't drink, but there was a bottle of Jose Cuervo—Frankie's favorite—in a bottom shelf in the kitchen.

We each took a shot with lime and salt. Frankie was in a class by herself when it came to holding her liquor and drugs. She could function at a high level, and she was a very good pool player. I could hold my acid, but one ounce of alcohol kicked my ass.

"I want a child with Bear," I announced as the tequila quickly dispersed to my tongue.

Frankie jumped and shrieked.

"He's smart, Frankie. He can solve any problem, and he has a photographic memory. He's a great choice for a father."

Frankie put her hands on her face and pulled in her beautiful cheeks before she spoke. "Who cares about smarts? Bear's too selfish. I am too. That's why I don't want children."

"I hear this calling, 'have a child, have a child.' Don't you have it?"

Frankie laughed so hard I thought she would crack a rib, and slapped her knee like a cowboy at a rodeo.

She took my head and kissed the top of it. "No, Rhoney. I don't hear that."

Her voice went husky. "I'm not a mother. I couldn't be me and a mother. It's not in the cards."

"But if you had a baby, you'd have big tits."

Frankie thought for a moment, perfectly serious. "No, I just want a man."

I turned up the tape of a recent Grateful Dead performance. She got up and danced. So did I. I mimicked her dance and the lightness of her movements.

"Mickey's taken up with this rich chick from New York City who has kids."

"I bet he's a soft mark for those kids."

"Wow, you got it. Of course he is. The Jensen girls live with him too."

Frankie shook her head. Mickey had brought her into the scene, but he was no longer her interest.

"How about Kreutzmann?"

"Susila wants to get pregnant."

Looking at Frankie, I decided to speak no more of babies and changed the music to a tape of Dark Star, playing it on Bear's Norelco cassette recorder. It did sound good.

I flopped back on the couch and ruminated, "I'm blown away by Hunter's lyrics, even if sometimes I don't get it. Like what does 'transitive nightfall of diamonds' mean? I ask Hunter and he won't tell me."

I played a recent version of Cosmic Charley. Frankie listened to the lyrics, trying to get all the words. "Kite on ice," she repeated, then jumped up and broke into a tap-dance-like routine. I loved watching her.

"How's Phil for you?" I asked, as if we had a checklist.

"Phil's too serious. No wonder Bear and he are such good friends."

"Isn't Bobby too young for you?"

I lowered the music volume. She joined me on the couch.

"He's got his serious side." Frankie and I looked into each other's eyes.

"Bear says Weir needs to take more LSD, but Bobby does what he wants."

"I like that he can stand up to Bear." Her voice got soft and low again. "Bobby's the real thing."

"He's not with anyone, really. He doesn't even have a place to live."

"I could fix that." She put her arms around me. "You just wait and see."

"He cut his hair."

Frankie looked shocked.

"Not short, don't worry, but it was too long." I felt almost maternal about Bobby. Maybe mothering him helped me mother myself.

Frankie hooted. I howled back. She and the tequila gave me self-confidence.

Frankie laughed. "Weir's so handsome, he can get away with any kind of hair."

Frankie jumped up again. She was high-spirited, like a thoroughbred horse.

We stepped outside into the cool night air. I took a skinny out of my cigarette case. I lit up my joint and she her ciggie. We sang together— "la dee dah, la dee dee dah."

We swung our bodies in time to our own rhythm, went inside and reclaimed our territory on the overstuffed couch.

"How's Bobby getting along with the band?" she questioned, looking thoughtful.

"Frankie, you want Bobby, don't you? 'Frankie Weir'! I like the sound of it."

Moving On: This Is a Bittersweet Tao*

Ramrod borrowed the Dead's white Dodge to move me to Marin. We stopped at the country store alongside the railroad tracks.

Ramrod said, "Get a gas can and fill it up here. Keep it in your Rambler's trunk."

"Isn't that dangerous?" I knew I sounded wimpy.

"No. Your gas gauge doesn't work and you're going to need it."

We drove to my new place. In the back of the house was a plot of land that would be perfect for a garden, but there was no fertile earth, only mud. Everyone had a garden. Even the egret had a fucking garden.

Ramrod stood by the inlet off the river under the eucalyptus tree and heard me.

"Sue Swanson lives on the other side of the tracks. She'll hook you up with good garden dirt."

I called her and she said, "We'll get soil delivered and manure. We're a stone's throw from Petaluma, the chicken capital of the world, and chicken shit is the best fertilizer."

In the river mud, I shaped a rectangle of soil and chicken shit, working it with a hoe. There was nothing to weed. Nothing grew in mud. I watched the egret and its mate standing motionless in the shallows as if they were waiting for me to get my shit together.

*I Ching

When Bear was on the road, I visited his house every third day to bring in the mail and feed Screech the owl. Babysitting Bear's owl was no easy task. Bear was proprietary toward the owl. Even after I showed him a light-blue speckled egg I had found in her cage, he had trouble calling him a her. The mouse fed to Screech had to be healthy and fresh because one time Screech had gotten sick from a stale mouse. So I went to the best pet store in Marin to select a good-looking mouse and went from there straight to Bear's house. I got the owl into the bathtub with the mouse and closed the door, knowing I would have to wait—sometimes as long as twelve hours—for the owl to stalk the mouse, break its neck, and eat it from the head down—all but the tail. The ritual was complete when the owl spit out a hair ball. To Owsley this was a sign of good digestion.

When Bear returned from the road, he called me. A letter had come to his post office box in Berkeley from the University of California with the state seal on the envelope. Should he open it?

"No," I said. "Bring it out here. I'll make you dinner. I've discovered a butcher in Novato who hangs his meat." Bear liked my house.

I opened up the envelope, and there it was—the acceptance letter to the UC Berkeley Graduate School of Education, beginning fall semester, 1969.

Robert Hunter Meets Owsleystein

At the Fillmore West, formerly the Carousel Ballroom, my nickname was Electric. I would share my LSD. I loved getting high. I was good at it. I had my freak-out early in the game, but after more than a hundred acid trips, my familiarization changed the experience. I still had hallucinatory visuals, but my free-associative inner thoughts were now the place of transformation. My self got high.

In 1969, on the night of June 7, I gyrated on the dance floor under the strobe light, losing myself in the rhythm section of the Grateful Dead. Then Janis Joplin came on stage and joined Pigpen for "Turn On Your Love Light."

"Turn on your love light," I screamed, inaudible in the ocean of amplified music.

Onstage Pigpen and Janis reveled in the lyrics and each other. On the floor, everyone danced with abandon. Bear appeared and gravitated to me. We moved in circles around each other, faster and faster.

The song ended, the house lights came on, and hundreds of stoned hippies looked for each other. We went backstage where Janis was sprawled on a velvet upholstered chair with her legs over the arm rest. The three-gallon stainless steel punch bowl on the table was empty. Wow, I thought. Bear had spiked the Kool-Aid with LSD and it was all gone. No wonder everyone was so stoned.

Janis sprang up from the chair, shook out her bell-bottoms, and angrily approached Bear.

"Man," she roared, "What the fuck did you put in that Kool-Aid?" She pointed her finger at Bear's face, her voice hoarse from singing. Her bracelets jangled. "My saxophone player is in the hospital. Your fucking Kool-Aid freaked him out. Man, you know these cats are studio musicians. They don't know from your fuckin' psychedelic scene."

Bear was suddenly sober enough to make sense of this onslaught.

"I put the usual in the Kool-Aid. If your sax man can't handle a little pure LSD, he might not be up to your standard."

Bear was still pissed at Janis for leaving Big Brother. He was convinced that Big Brother had been a better band.

Janis was insulted. "He's a great sax man, and now he's in the hospital overdosed on your fuckin' LSD."

"What did he do—drink half the bowl?" Bear twittered provocatively.

Janis and Bear argued—two confrontational Capricorns who shared a January 19 birthday. Bear explained with his usual dose, 270 micrograms, drinking a glassful, as most people did, was ideal. Still, how much Kool-Aid is in a punchbowl? Bear would have put his aluminum briefcase down on the table with assorted cookies, paper cups, and the punchbowl. Opening his bountiful man-purse, he would have pulled out a glassine paper bindle of crystalline LSD and added a measure to the punchbowl like a chef adding stock to the soup du jour. As he had on other occasions, he might have stirred the liquid with his finger, then put it in his mouth, testing the taste for the slightly acerbic presence of lysergic acid.

"With more than a cup, you'd have a sugar meltdown. The insulin release is worse on your system," Bear declared.

"The dose in a glass of punch is too small to send your sax man to the hospital. Something else must have happened."

"A lot of people got too stoned," someone joined in.

Bear questioned a few prominent entities backstage and found that Goldfinger had been there before the show. "He must have spiked the Kool-Aid too. What an asshole. He didn't even check with me."

Owsley was furious but continued to methodically pack up the equipment. When we were ready to leave, no one was left in the ballroom except Bill Graham standing on the stairway with his arms crossed. Owsley was vexed but silent as we slid past and out the door. The night air was cold and clear. The stars were out and beckoning. The music was still playing in my head. My feet barely touched the ground.

"Let's go to OJ's for a steak."

"Good," I answered. "I'm hungry, too."

The street was deserted. Then I heard a moan, a guttural utterance as if an animal were in distress. At first I thought I was hallucinating, but then I heard it again. It seemed to come from below. I saw a naked human form, flesh and hair lying in the gutter. I bent closer and recognized Robert Hunter's face. He was dirty, distressed, muttering to himself.

When Bear walked up, Hunter jumped to his feet. "Owsleystein!" He grabbed Bear in a headlock.

"Hunter," I cried, "What are you doing? That's Bear."

He acted like he couldn't hear me and responded, "I will annihilate you, Owsleystein!"

Bear was trying not to struggle with his freaked-out friend.

"The monster you created destroyeth you."

Hunter was bulky and strong, and I pulled at his arm around Bear's neck, and suddenly he fell to the ground.

His eyes were wide and so dilated I couldn't see their color. Bear got away and quietly walked in the direction of the car. I stood by the stricken poet.

"No, Bear, we can't leave Hunter like this."

Bear stopped in his tracks and stared at the sidewalk, his hands clenched at his sides. "Fuck it! Now we can't go to Original Joe's. Let's take Hunter to Goldfinger's house. I'll get the car."

Hunter was speaking in his deep voice of dire predictions, dreaded consequences, crackups, and wrecks. He was in a time warp, an alternate reality on Market Street. Hunter thought I was sharing his vision, but I had no idea what planet he was on. I knew enough not to drink from an open punch bowl. My own supply had given me the choice of how high I wanted to be. To me Hunter looked like a prehistoric man, a Neanderthal, as he lay down once more in the gutter on Market Street. I couldn't help staring at his penis.

"Hunter," I asked, "Where are your clothes?"

He pointed. About thirty feet further up the street were his jeans, white briefs, socks, and boots. Here was the poet who translated Rilke's poetry, the intellectual who embraced the philosophy of Edmund Husserl, believing that perception alters fact. Boy, was he dusted.

I offered him his jeans. "Put on your clothes!"

He accepted the pants, then threw them into the street. "Don't tell me what to do. You are not my mother."

He was right. I was being judgmental and critical at a time when love was needed. I had fallen back into old behavior patterns from my own fucked-up mother. I had not transformed. Oy vey iz mir.

Bear pulled up in the car. I opened the door to the back seat. "Hunter, come on. Get in."

Hunter looked at me without recognition. Bear helped me get Hunter on his feet but he resisted, pointing his finger at Bear, howling, "Owsleystein."

"Hunter does not want to come with us. Let's go."

"No, Bear. We can't leave him here." I stood before the caveman and looked into his eyes. "Hunter, it's Rhoney, Rhoney. See, me." I took his hand and tapped it on my head. "You can't stay on the street. It's late. The gig is over. Everyone's gone."

His face became the mask of tragedy. "She's gone," he moaned, tears welling.

"Hunter, what's the matter? Is it Christie you've lost?" He shook his head yes. He and his gorgeous girlfriend were inseparable. Where *was* she?

"Don't worry. We'll find her. Come with us now. Hunter, please," I pleaded. "Get into the car. We'll look for Christie. I promise. Everything will be okay. Come on, baby. 'Come on baby, do the locomotion.'" I sung to him in my raspy voice and wiggled my butt like a choo-choo train. My voice soothed him enough to get him into the backseat.

Bear drove in his haphazard fashion through a maze of back streets until we pulled up in front of Goldfinger's Victorian flat on Nob Hill. Hunter was crouched down and quiet, but when the engine stopped he wailed, "She always will be in the shadow of my heart. Where, where did she go?"

"Hunter, it's okay. We'll find her."

"Hunter's a Cancer. He can't help worrying about his home and family," observed Bear. "Let's dump him on Goldfinger."

Hunter was a big guy and it was a struggle to get him halfway up the long stairway to Goldfinger's front door. I held up Hunter as Bear scrambled to the top and returned with Goldfinger's girl, Nicki. Goldfinger wasn't there, but Nicki was cool. The three of us guided Hunter up the remaining climb, his deep voice calling out, "Gone," as we made it inside.

Nicki said, "She could be at Garcia's. I'll call out there."

Hunter sat on the sofa by the bay window looking out at the Golden Gate Bridge. He shook his head. "No, no!"

Nicki frisked her long brown hair off her face as she sat before the heavy black telephone on the table. She concentrated on the matter at hand. The babysitter answered. No, Mountain Girl and Garcia were not home. No Christie.

"We need to talk to Goldfinger. Someone at the Airplane house will know where he is." Bear sat next to Nicki, commandeered the phone, and called, but no Goldfinger.

Hunter pointed at Bear. "Owsleystein!" Then his arm fell back and he stared at the Persian carpet.

"I think he's better," Owsley said.

"Hunter," I asked, "Would you like some water?"

No answer. I went into the kitchen and brought back a glass of water. I handed Hunter the heavy, ornate glass. He eyed it suspiciously and gave it back. Nicki propped a pillow behind him, and he slumped on the couch. She joined me at the table. Bear rummaged through the refrigerator, looking for food, ruminating on his options, "Rabbit food. Nothing but rabbit food." He turned to us. "Where is Goldfinger? I hope he just put acid in that Kool-Aid. But with Goldfinger, you never know." Bear chuckled.

I realized I was getting hungry, too. I found bread, cereal, milk, and bananas. Comfort food was just fine with me.

"Carbs, nothing but carbs," Bear commented. "There's nothing to eat."

I contradicted him. "There's a jar of peanut butter."

"Where?"

"The second shelf on the door."

Just then Hunter walked in and ranted about the way reality looked to him, "Only perception gives an object dimension that the mind creates. I am not your creation. I am not your trip. I control my presentation in time. You only control your perception of me."

I was still very high myself. I was in that clear mental state when the mind feels like a planet-sized chamber. "Hunter," I asked, engaging his thought processes, "is it the viewer's perception of consciousness, not consciousness itself, which is critical?"

Suddenly Hunter looked happy.

"It is not the object but the perception of the object. There are distinctions and there are connections." I felt as if I finally had done something to help. I smiled too.

But just as quickly, Hunter returned to the darkness; his words became incoherent. He dropped to the couch, put his hands over his mouth, and became lachrymose.

Nicki suggested taking Hunter to the hospital, but Bear and I knew that was a bad idea. In hospitals, they put freak-outs on Thorazine.

"Thorazine is the wrong way to go," Bear said, "but niacinamide—it sometimes works. I've got some here, I think."

Niacinamide is a B vitamin that has antianxiety effects. In 1956, Abram Hoffer, one of Bear's heroes, a Canadian biochemist and MD, had successfully reversed all LSD symptoms by intravenously injecting one gram of niacinamide into subjects high on LSD; however, the government quashed LSD research before the start of clinical trials. Bear went to his aluminum briefcase and produced a bottle of 500-milligram pills.

"Works better if injected, not well absorbed enterally, but . . ." Bear counted out five.

Hunter was so weak, I helped him put the pills in his mouth, but suddenly he leaped up, spit out the pills, and lunged at me like a cornered caveman.

"Hunter's not listening to us, but he'll listen to Garcia. Call again, Nicki."

Nicki got on the phone and Garcia answered. Help on the way.

"Owsleystein," Hunter shouted.

Nicki turned her head away from the telephone and grinned. "Garcia heard that. He says, 'Owsleystein' is a perfect name for Bear."

Now if only Christie would show up.

At that moment Goldfinger burst into the room, his red hair flaming like a halo around his rosy face and pointed nose. He was dressed like a pirate satyr. His green velvet shirt was cuffed above his ruby-inlaid claw, which he used to remove his Stetson.

Bear took him by the arm and led him to the table. "What did you put in the punch?"

"Your crystal LSD."

We all breathed a sigh of relief.

"Asshole. You should have talked to me first." Goldfinger carried the crystal in a brown medicine bottle. They calculated that between them 1 gram of LSD got into the Kool-Aid: 4,000 hits of LSD were poured into forty cups of Kool-Aid, meaning that in one cup of that double-dosed Kool-Aid was 3,000 to 5,000 micrograms of LSD. True, that was only 3 to 5 milligrams, which for most drugs is a miniscule amount. A standard dose of LSD to bring on visual and auditory hallucinations was 270 micrograms. Taking 5,000 micrograms was some new kind of record. Too bad Bill Graham didn't get it, I thought. He's the one who needed it.

"That Kool-Aid was worth $50,000 on the street," Goldfinger laughed.

"Is Hunter going to be all right?" I worried.

Bear said his trip would go on for another day and his perception of time and sense limitation would be distorted. The whole experience would be profound but not damaging to his organs and physiologic systems. His normal faculties would return.

The sun came up, and Garcia arrived with Hunter's favorite English wool coat and helped him on with it. They sat together on the couch, neither of them talking. Garcia put his arm around Hunter. Hunter did not react. Silence. Garcia opened up his guitar case with a loud snap. When Garcia played the guitar, Hunter perked up. I gave him the niacinamide, and he carefully swallowed each pill with a sip of water. He was dehydrated.

Nicki stood up, "Anyone for pancakes?"

Garcia chuckled, "Buckwheat dollars—sure. Whaddya say, Hunter? Could ya go for a stack?" Hunter smiled.

Bear proclaimed, "Carbs. I would rather not eat." He continued to eat the entire jar of peanut butter.

Hunter was coming down, but he was angry at Bear and emotional about Christie. She showed up a day later with a wild story about abduction and escape, and soon after made plans to move to London.

My mind had picked up Hunter's hallucination, and I was haunted by the sense that reality was established by perception. If I changed my perception, I could change my reality. I could have eaten pancakes—been the witness and the witnessed.

Don't drink from an open punch bowl.

Woodstock 1969

By the time we were close enough to hear the sounds of distant music, it was night. The limo was dark and the air-conditioning was on. No one said much. Garcia and Nicki were seated opposite me. Ahead of us, on the one road leading into the site, cars were slowly making their way. Behind us cars were backed up as far as the eye could see. We were moving very slowly through a light rain.

I had already lost Bear. Intent on discussing his electronic modifications for Jack's bass, he had gotten into the Jefferson Airplane's limo with Jack and Melissa. I was on my own.

It stopped raining when we arrived. At the Welcome Tent, we were greeted by Jonathan Reister. Frankie and I called him "the Cowboy" not just because of the hat and boots but because of the way he sweet-talked us when he flirted, as if he were talking to his horse.

"The sleeping bags are coming," he drawled. He was working with Wavy Gravy and the Hog Farm, setting up a tent for the Grateful Dead. He beckoned me into an office. He pulled the curtain closed. In his hand was a rolled-up hundred-dollar bill and a packet of cocaine. We snorted the cocaine. He lowered his pants. He wore no underwear. My heart beat rapidly when I looked at him. I needed attention and pulled him to me. This opportunity had to be taken.

Garcia's head popped through the curtain. He saw me with the Cowboy, clucked in disapproval, and disappeared. I felt guilty. Garcia had stipulated that if I came to Woodstock, I had to stay with Bear. Outside, I heard Bear's voice grumbling that the tents should have been set up and the camping gear there. I left the Cowboy struggling with his jeans, stumbled out of the tent, and took my place beside Bear. Let Garcia see Bear and me. From the distant stage, Joan Baez was singing, her clear lucid tones penetrating the cloudy air. Huge applause swelled at the end of her set.

Bear had wandered off, dispensing acid to whoever said yes, and if anyone said no, convincing them that they meant yes. Garcia went to the motel. Frankie and Weir were lost in each other. Phil chose the campgrounds and climbed into a sleeping bag. When it was time to make a decision about where to spend the night. I crawled into one of the sleeping bags and stripped off my clothes. "Good night, Phil," I said and passed out.

In the morning the sun was shining. Although the ground was still damp, the day was beautiful.

"Let's head for the lakes," Phil suggested.

"Okay," I said. We set off through the sea of mud and hippies. I kept congratulating myself that I brought clogs as they were perfect foot protection for this environment. Phil wasn't so lucky in his canvas tennis loafers.

Bear appeared before us with his Murine bottle, and I took a drop under the tongue. If he knew about my indiscretion, he didn't say so. He cupped my butt with his hands and hugged me. We were still a perfect fit.

"Coming for a swim, man?" Phil asked Bear, who was hopping up and down, pointing at the equipment, moving toward the stage. He mumbled something about work and disappeared in the opposite direction.

Phil and I were simply two more hippies trudging through the mud, headed for the lakes. The LSD was coming on. It seemed as if the whole Earth had become the festival.

We found a lake with big rocks. Hippies were skinny dipping. Phil and I looked at each other, ripped off our clothes, counted "1, 2, 3," and jumped into the cold water. It was an awakening.

I submerged myself in the lake, and the water soothed and cleaned me.

I did not want to carry regrets, but many times I did not have right action.

I shouldn't have screwed around with The Cowboy and cocaine, but I did. I thought, I need to forgive myself. Let it go! I'm another happy hippie skinny dipping at the Woodstock Music Festival.

Phil's long lanky body was sexy, and he floated on top of the water, relaxing. His blonde hair stuck to his skin. The sun came out and the Catskill Mountain lake sparkled. It was slippery climbing out of the water onto the rock. He went first and helped me up. We lay down to dry in the August sun. We could see the clouds coming. We were so different—his Aryan body and my Jewish one. I could confide in Phil. He reminded me of my brother, both Pisces, both Phil. My brothers had been bar mitzvahed near Woodstock with all the trappings of a big Jewish party, but I had only felt embarrassment.

Dark clouds streamed in and covered the sun. "Must be almost time for us to go on," said Phil as he put on his clothes.

We headed back for the stage through the milling herds of hippies, nude and clothed, splashing in mud puddles, dancing to the music.

Before the Grateful Dead went on, the rain came down again and the ground turned to sloshy mud. Bear and Ramrod and the crew were loading equipment on one of the three revolving stages, but as they loaded the heavy McIntosh tube amps, the stage began to sink from the weight of the equipment.

"Bear," I shouted from the side of the stage, "The stage is collapsing." I really was worried, but he ignored me. Oblivious to the danger, Bear was plugging in cables, setting up microphone stands and mics, followed by Ramrod, who shadowed him. They worked without talking.

Garcia had waited long enough and took the stage. The crowd roared in anticipation. Bear bitched, "Not yet, not yet, we're not ready. The equipment isn't grounded. There's a sixty-cycle hum coming through the sound system."

Bobby Weir approached his microphone and a spark shot out, arced, and hit him in the lip. He jumped back in pain. Frankie screamed, "Are you okay?" He comforted her and laughed, but his lip had been burned.

The dampness made the strings go out of tune. "Dark Star," solely instrumental, sounded off. They played for about a half hour and cut the set short. Garcia was the first to leave the stage. He nearly threw his guitar to Ramrod.

Bear was bummed. He cornered Phil and complained that the set was too short, that he was just ironing out the wrinkles in the sound system when the band stopped playing.

Before I could ask Bear about our sleeping arrangements, he was gone. I wondered what I should do. I was in a psychedelic state and saw my circumstances as a lesson in nonduality—the acceptance of gain and loss as the same. Life felt full in his presence and when he wasn't there.

Phil and I had shared that moment. We both got it.

By the end of The Who's set, Bear was still nowhere to be found.

Phil said, "I'll get you on the helicopter."

I accepted his offer. We walked directly to the helicopter port, avoiding the crowd, and without any hassles got on the helicopter. I dutifully took a seat and strapped myself in. The helicopter lifted through jeweled curtains into dark space.

I felt so thankful to Phil, but what could I offer? All I had was sex and Phil did not want that from me. I pulled out my notebook and wrote him a poem.

> I was able to see
> by seeing you
> by seeing my image reflected in your eyes
> vibrating in the sound of your voice
> coming out of your fingers.
> Your acceptance of me and you and us
> is the triad of divinity
> the holy trinity.
> We are part of the whole
> manifesting the music
> listening to the music
> hearing the silence.
> The transformation takes work.
> On the side of the hill
> deep in the ravine
> at a Catskill lake
> we see the face of love
> in each other.
> Our bodies are inspired creations
> of atoms scattering and reforming.
> I lean into you.
> You flow into my curve
> and support me.

You teach me how to be part of you.
You teach me how to be myself.

When we got to the motel, I slipped the poem in his pocket. There were not enough rooms for everyone to have their own, and Bear and Mickey were assigned a room to share. Bear apparently had shown up at some point during the day. Mickey's room had two double beds, and I put down my stuff. He was in bed with Cookie, who didn't want me to share their motel room. I told her to shut the fuck up, stripped down, and without brushing my teeth or putting Dr. Hauschka's rose cream on my face, I crawled into the other bed.

In what seemed like no time, it was morning and the sun was out. I jumped out of bed and threw on my clothes, determined not to miss another minute of Woodstock. I would find Bear; he was out there. Writing the poem had freed me. I headed back to the helicopter pad to get a ride to the site. As early as it was, Garcia was there with Nicki bundled up in a wool serape.

"Where's Bear?" Garcia asked.

I shrugged my shoulders. "I haven't seen him."

"You are supposed to stay with Bear. That was our agreement. You can't get on the helicopter unless you're with Bear."

"I can't be with Bear. He's not here."

"Then you shouldn't be here. That's the point!" Garcia turned away from me.

The sound of the helicopter was deafening. The pilot opened the hatch for the passengers. I just got on the helicopter and Garcia let it go. We all looked down at the sea of humanity gathered for the Woodstock Festival, like wee folk at a pagan festival.

"Bear's down there somewhere . . . squirting drops under hippie tongues."

"Owsley acid is the best," Nicki added, in her intuitive way diverting the conversation from further bullshit. We were all together, we were all vulnerable. We were all cool.

When the helicopter landed we walked to the stage. At stage left, Weir was dancing energetically to Canned Heat, "Ya got no money, ya got no home . . ." His hair was long again and wild. He was grinning.

Crosby, Stills, Nash, and Young took the stage. Melissa and Jack were standing at the side, and I joined them. Bear appeared from behind me and fondled my breasts under my shirt.

"Where have you been?" I started to scold, but he planted a wet kiss on my lips and shut me up. "Um," I hummed. "More. I like."

"Open your mouth."

I did what I was told.

Grace and Paul Kantner were next to Jack. They opened their mouths like a nest full of baby birds, and Bear fed all the little birdie heads. The Band was singing, "We are four for each other." Magic! I danced. Many voices harmonized to make a fuller sound. We were family.

As the sun came up, Jimi Hendrix played the "Star Spangled Banner." Everyone spontaneously stopped and faced the stage and listened. It was the moment of becoming.

I woke up in the motel room when the door opened and Bear and Ramrod came in. They opened the blinds and the sun streamed in. In five minutes, we were in the limo headed to the airport. On the plane, I barely spoke. Bear crashed. He had been up the entire festival. Ramrod was in the seat next to me, and it was easy not to talk. He hardly ever spoke. I leaned my head on his shoulder. He took off his green Woodstock T-shirt and put it around me. With Ramrod I felt comfortable. The combination of us was expanded consciousness. This was the best I'd ever had and I wasn't letting go.

Hippie needs a miracle   © *Alvan Meyerowitz*

Fathers

My father decided to visit me in California to celebrate my birthday. He flew out to San Francisco and called me from his hotel, the Mark Hopkins at the crest of Nob Hill. We met early and had a great dinner at his hotel restaurant, the Top of the Mark, with 360-degree views of the Bay and the Pacific. The next day he called and said he wanted to see my house, but I said, no, I'd meet him at Point Reyes. I didn't want him snooping at my home in Black Point, even with Bear on the road. Any evidence of my private life was ammunition for my father. He rented a car and I met him at the beach. We walked in the sand. We looked at the gray waters of the Pacific. I talked to him about my life and read him a poem I had written.

> I am free, like the waves, hitting the beach
> I feel the roughness of the touch
> And the freedom of the expression
> At the same time
> Together
> I know I am weird, wired weird.
> We treat each other to the joy of acknowledgment.

I had taken about 270 micrograms that morning. I had my personal stash of liquid LSD in a brown glass bottle that I sometimes wrapped in aluminum foil. My father asked me about Bear. I said nothing. My father could never understand how I could love Bear, how I could be part of a nonmonogamous relationship. I couldn't tell him that my mother's criticism still disturbed me deeply.

He said, "You're mother is the one who wanted me to visit you."

How typical! My mother didn't have the balls to contact me, and my father would rather be in his dental office. Not really—the old mensch did love me.

I had invited my boss, Lenny Hart, and Mickey, his son and Grateful Dead drummer, to have dinner with Father and me but Mickey was on the road. Lenny insisted we join him for a revival meeting. He drove us in his new American car, his new big blonde wife beside him. In the back with my father I was short and so low in the seat, I had no idea where we were going. My father was short too.

Lenny parked in front of a tract house in a suburban neighborhood. Where was the revival tent? We went immediately to the backyard. Lenny nodded and people bowed as we headed toward the front, past rows of seats filled with people cheering. My father smiled broadly and followed Lenny, saying "hello" and nodding his head. Toward the front, we took seats, but almost immediately Lenny got up and addressed the crowd of about a hundred people.

A man with a short-sleeved white shirt and a hat yelled, "The Reverend Lenny Hart!" My father clapped.

"Like Jesus, the meek shall inherit the Earth," the Reverend Lenny Hart preached. My father clapped again.

Lenny's wife uttered, "Amen."

A large white woman put her hands up in the air. "I went down to my Lord and He lifted me up."

My father said, "Tell it, sister."

My father was a religious man in the Jewish tradition. He did not work on Saturday. On Saturday he went to synagogue. Every day of his adult life, he wrapped straps of leather up and down his arms in prayer because at the age of thirteen, he promised his grandfather he would do the daily tefillin practice. He volunteered his services at hospital clinics two days a week. Now he was cheering testimonials at a revival meeting.

I was turned off but relieved that my father was having a good time. He was socializing with my friends.

"Rho*ney*," he said emphasizing the sound of my name as if I were a nay, a nothing. "Why don't you get up there and tell your story? Talk about your addiction to drugs."

My consciousness spun out of control. I turned my head back and forth trying to clear my brain. I heard the voice of Lenny Hart crack through my confusion.

"Are you sure you want to do that, Rhoney?" Lenny Hart was kinder than my dad at this moment.

"Yes." My father touched me. "GET UP THERE."

Like the chameleon Kesey recognized in me, I shimmied up to the stage, moving as if possessed by a spirit, and at as high a pitch as I could muster I shouted to the assemblage, "I feel the spirit!"

"Amen, sister," came a familiar voice.

I continued, "And if it weren't for the Reverend Lenny Hart, we wouldn't be here now."

The place went wild with worship, and I shrunk into the background.

I said good-bye to my father like we were on good terms. He bought into that—one minute spite, the next love.

At Alembic, I had a desk, a telephone, and a typewriter. In 1969, the band had very little money and a lot of

work to fulfill their recording contract obligations.
Hunter and Garcia were writing new songs constantly.
Robert Hunter would ask me to type up his handwritten
scraps of lyrics. The songs had no titles. One of his new
songs was based on an old mine story of miraculous
rescue that I remembered from a Peggy Seeger folk song.
Also on that 1957 record was "Come All Ye Fair and
Tender Ladies," and another of my favorite songs, "I
Never Will Marry." But Hunter wasn't interested in my
favorite tunes. He wrote a line: "Annie Beauneu from
Saint Angel." Who the fuck is that, I wanted to ask, but
we had already established a formula. I did not read the
words. I typed. My job was secretary, not interpreter.
I was not allowed to ask for any definitions. "Never
mention meaning," he ordered me.

My other work was typing for Lenny Hart. Lenny's
job, as the Grateful Dead's official manager, was to control
expenses and make contacts for high-paying gigs. Lenny
dictated business letters to me: "To Whom It May Concern,
colon. Put the date first, Rhoney, and center properly."

I was a slow typist, and my real lack of secretarial skills
annoyed Lenny, who was seated at a desk directly behind
me. We were in a cavernous warehouse and our desks
were scrunched together. As usual, Lenny was on the
telephone. He put his hand over the receiver and boomed
at me, "Are you finished yet? How long does one page take
to type?"

Lenny had turned his back to the room and was facing
the window. He had a heavy wooden chair with wheels, and
his butt took up the entire seat. His shirt stretched tightly
over his back. When Mickey came in with drumsticks and his
rubber practice pad, he sat beside Lenny's desk and tapped
out a rhythm. One minute Lenny was brooding and angry,

and the next, he was a happy little kid. Bear had told me to watch out for him.

My stomach hurt and I grabbed my bag and rushed to the primitive bathroom adjacent to the office. I was late for my period and cramping. I locked the bathroom door and examined my underpants. No bright red blood. Not even a spot. That was weird. I was never late. I did the calculation in my head.

After my seminar in Educational Theory, I drove to the Oakland Hills house, thinking that it was really the lack of population control that made public education more concerned with the group than the individual. And here I was—pregnant! Bear and Ramrod were in the kitchen. "Ya want something to eat?"

I made a face and shook my head no.

"I'm nauseous. I'm sick to my stomach." I placed my hand on my belly and stuck out my chest. My tits were looking big. Big tits, erect nipples—the first sign!

"I'm—" I began.

Bear was eager to respond, and I thought for sure he got it, that he'd say something nice. "Too much driving," he exclaimed. "I told you not to go to school. You live in Black Point and drive to the East Bay several times a week. No wonder you don't feel well. That Nash Rambler is a great car—solid and stable on the road—it's built like a Sherman tank, perfect for you, but the way you drive . . . " He laughed as if it were a playground joke. It hurt my feelings and pushed my buttons all in one stroke.

"Are you calling me a bad driver? That's like the pot calling the kettle black. You're going to get into a terrible accident. You're the worst driver because your ego drives too fast!" I sat down.

There was no winning with Bear. He was such a sophist.

I could up the ante, like my mother, but I let it go. I couldn't talk to him and he couldn't listen. He was dismissive, and he never remembered the times when I was right.

I turned to Ramrod and he quietly put his arms around me, not a hug—more like shelter from a storm.

The next day, I was preoccupied. "As above, so below," Bear's voice said in my head.

As I walked into the office, Lenny yelled at me, "You're two hours late."

Hunter came into the room, saw I was upset, and cocked his head, "Stay cool. Don't let him get to you."

Lenny leaned on my desk with his elbows and onion breath. "The morning is when we make contacts with the promoters and do the band's business."

I moved back in my chair, startled by the confrontation. "What do you want me to do, Lenny?"

"Get on the phone right now." Lenny dictated a number in the southern California area code.

I did what he told me. The man on the other end said, "We do not want to book the Grateful Dead," and hung up.

I turned to Lenny and repeated the words. He glared at me, and his voice turned mean.

"What kind of secretary are you? You ruined the deal!"

I burst into tears and blurted out, "I'm pregnant!" As soon as the words were out of my mouth, I regretted it. Lenny rushed over to me and hugged me. "You poor baby. You're not even married. I bet you don't even know who the father is."

I left Alembic early. I could barely keep my eyes open. Of all the people in the world to tell I was pregnant, I tell Lenny Hart! I hadn't even told Bear.

The stars were out over the river flats. I was having difficulty putting one foot in front of the other. I made it

up the short flight of stairs to my bedroom and lay down
in my bed. My left eye could see out the window. In the
swamp, the egrets stood on one leg, motionless. The colors
seemed like negatives of photographs.

I dreamed I was in a sinking boat on a river of sorrow.
When I woke up my thighs were wet. A rumble cascaded
inside me and I fell onto the floor, curled into a ball, and
rolled around, as if to put out the fire, but the rolling
and the rocking could not ease the pain. I heard myself
scream. It was morning. I saw blood on the floor. I lay
in my baby's bloodbath. The phone rang. I crawled to
answer it and moaned hello. It was Lenny Hart. He said
was going for morning prayers and he was putting me and
the baby in his prayers. I groaned and gasped, "There is
no baby."

His condo on Lucas Valley Road was close by. He
arrived at Black Point at the same time as the ambulance.
He watched the EMS guys carry me out on a stretcher and
followed the ambulance to the hospital in his car. I was
seeing red. I passed out and dreamed of a lover holding me
aloft and caressing my body. He kissed every part of me
and rubbed away my fear. He was my companion in love.

I woke up in a hospital bed swathed in white sheets.
I squirmed and jerked to get free of the swaddles and
screamed when the pain hit me.

A nurse rushed in, alarmed. "You'll disengage your IV
line if you don't stay still."

"Why the pain?"

I clutched my belly.

"My dear child, you've had curettage, scraping. After
a miscarriage, you must have a D and C, dilation and
curettage, to clean out residual tissue in the uterus, if you
want to conceive again."

The next day Lenny Hart picked me up and drove me home. As he turned into my gravel driveway, Kidd Candelario came out the front door. Kidd did not like Lenny.

"Howdy-doo Reverend Hart! Save any souls today?" Kidd was sarcastic and mean. Lenny did not come in.

Kidd had moved into the bedroom downstairs and he was real worried about me. That was a switch. I was usually the one worried about him. He was barely sixteen but foul mouthed and swaggering. His real name was William. He had left home very young. Mention parents to him and he shut down. He was uneducated and uninterested. Moving dope was what he wanted to do, and he had it all mapped out. Southern California, Laguna Beach, he'd surf and smuggle and live his dream.

He would take care of me. He filled the refrigerator with cheese, meat, and tortillas. His favorite thing was tacos. He'd chop the lettuce and grate the cheese, fry up the meat and chile, place the whole deal on a tortilla directly on the burner, and toast it.

"You look awful. Eat." He handed me a taco. My teeth crunched when I bit down on the food. I had dry mouth from anesthesia and hospital drugs. I lay on the couch opposite the kitchen. I was anemic.

Kidd put his hand on my head and reassured me. "I have to do my job at the Fillmore. It will be late, but I'll come back here. You won't be alone."

He closed the door and I fell into a deep sleep.

Rolling Stones Live, 1969

I was still not completely recovered, but I wasn't going to miss The Rolling Stones concert. I staggered to my closet and pulled out a leather skirt and cowboy shirt and boots. In my head I planned my strategy. I would tell Bear I wanted a child.

Lenny Hart picked me up and we drove to the
Oakland Coliseum. The front seat of his car was roomy
and I stretched out in comfort, but our "seats" at the show,
although they were front and center, were uncomfortable
metal benches. The floors reverberated with a tinny sound
from thousands of feet.

There's no way to dance, I thought. Just as well for
me, hunched over in pain, smack in the middle of the
row. Pigpen swaggered in with his woman, Vee, who sat
on the other side of Lenny. Garcia came with Mountain
Girl, who greeted me and continued chatting to Jerry.
Frankie and Weir held hands. Finally the rest of the band
straggled in and we filled up half a row. Phil took the end
seat, his long legs stretching into the aisle. The Ike and
Tina Turner Band opened the show. She was so hot, no
one could outdo her, except The Rolling Stones.

When the lights came up and The Stones took the stage,
the audience went wild. Everyone was on their feet. The
spotlight focused on Mick Jagger as he broke into "Jumping
Jack Flash" and pranced up and down the stage. Seated, I
clutched my belly as the cramps began, but the music was
so wonderful, it took away the pain. When The Stones
played, "I'm free to do what I want, any old time," I had to
dance. This was my tune. The stadium floor rumbled like
an earthquake. Everyone was up and moving except Lenny.

We stayed for the next set. There seemed to be a
commotion on stage and a long lapse before the second
set. At one point, I thought I saw Bear crouched down
next to Phil, but before I could scramble past Lenny and
get his attention, he was gone. Around midnight, in the
middle of a song, in the dark, Lenny Hart took me by the
hand and pulled me with him to the exit.

e-mail from bear to me

```
November, 2006: Re: Rolling Stones, Novem-
ber 9, 1969
They blew all their Ampeg speakers by the
end of their first set. RR, Sonny Hurd and
Jackson ran over to the old Fillmore where
we had played the night before and were
scheduled to play the next night. They were
able to return just in time to loan them our
stuff for their second set (I am sure they
were grateful, but they all said they did
not like the "Fender sound"—I was amazed—I
thought their Ampegs sucked—big time). I
was allowed to (secretly) plug my little
cassette machine into the PA for their sec-
ond set. I still have the cassette, but the
machine was running 6% slow.
```

Altamont, December 6, 1969

To celebrate the success of their US tour, The Rolling Stones agreed to play for free with the San Francisco psychedelic rock bands, and the Grateful Dead volunteered to organize the event. Where would we hold this free show? Location, location, location. Bear had predicted that "permits" were problematic for the authorities, and even before the first big planning meeting, Golden Gate Park was ruled out. All San Francisco was out. The committee met at Alembic.

Emmett Grogan, a Digger, was always involved if a free event were in the works. The Diggers made sure everyone had food, clothing, shelter, and basic rights. Before there was performance art, they started the San Francisco Mime Troupe. Free outdoor theater was their domain and joy. On a street corner, they would build a theater from a small platform and a velvet curtain. Now the police chose to deny permits to these anarchist hippies and closed down street theater. Emmett, the bad boy of the 1960s, was handsome and compelling in conversation, but he had an epileptic seizure at Alembic and fell on the concrete floor writhing and foaming at the mouth in front of all of us, afterward remembering nothing. He could not be in charge.

Rock Scully represented the Grateful Dead, despite Bear's objection to his choice of narcotics; and Sam Cutler, The Stones' road manager, MC, and all-purpose point man, was emissary for The Rolling Stones.

Bear told me Melvin Belli, the high-profile San Francisco personal injury attorney, had cut a deal and we had Sears Point Raceway. Bear was enthusiastic. "Sears Point Raceway is only twenty minutes from Alembic. We can provide the sound system. We can record with the 16-track."

He called Terry the Tramp. When the Grateful Dead did free outdoor shows, the Hell's Angels showed up and acted as "security" and crowd control. They usually parked their bikes next to the generators. Everyone knows you can't touch an Angel's bike. Terry the Tramp arrived at Alembic and made it clear that Sears Point was not his club's territory; jurisdiction is sacred among Angels.

Sam Cutler very seriously addressed us in the office at Alembic: The location was top secret. Don't tell anybody. Of course, everybody already knew.

My secretarial phone rang nonstop. It seemed that someone had leaked Sears Point as the location, and the owner, having second thoughts about half a million people stampeding to hear Mick Jagger, pulled the permit.

Sam Cutler threw a fit. We worked the phones constantly—negotiating, cajoling, wheedling, calling in all

our comps, consulting with lawyers—and finally, once again
the head honcho, Melvin Belli, found the location. "Stop
calling," Sam ordered. "We got it! Altamont Speedway."

Altamont sat on the San Andreas Fault, and the
Greenville and Tesla Faults, near the Lawrence Livermore
National Laboratory, the largest research center for lethal
weaponry, in an otherwise barren and abandoned landscape.

Ultimately, it was the only option still open. The show
must go on.

Terry the Tramp warned, "Hell's Angels in Livermore
are not what you're used to."

I looked at Sam; he was somewhere else. He was English.

The stage crew dismantled the speaker towers they'd
just built at Sears Point and reloaded the trucks. Bear was
spending his own money to move his equipment. He was
the last to leave. He did not sleep. He had no time to give
away LSD for the concert. He was 100% focused on the
sound. No Owsley acid for Altamont. Suffer.

Helicopters carried the musicians to the venue from
the heliport in Sausalito and I took the first ride over.
The Altamont landscape was wrong for a rock'n'roll
show but perfect for landing helicopters. They came in
and out. Sound equipment arrived on trucks; a hundred
cases of beer were stacked near the stage; Porta-Potties
were delivered. All night the crew worked under glaring
highway construction spotlights. Bear crawled over the
sound system like an ant in a colony. We thought we
could duplicate the spirit of Woodstock, but the setting of
Altamont was not the Catskills. There was no right place
to put the stage. The land was too flat and the stage was
too low, level with the audience, no natural amphitheater
shaping up here. The Rolling Stones were traveling with
a film crew, and many unfamiliar people were backstage.

Trucks were moved to the backstage area as protection and the Hell's Angels' bikes ringed the front of the stage. As if this were enough.

The Jefferson Airplane was the third band. Sam Cutler introduced them with his usual fanfare. I was at the side of the stage when a Livermore Hell's Angel knocked out Marty Balin while he was almost finished singing the first song. He had unwisely jumped between the Angel and the rowdy audience member who pushed over his Harley. Sam implored the masses to stay calm.

It was time for the Dead to go on, but Bill, Mickey, Jerry, Bob, and Phil huddled together and decided not to play. Something was off. The vibe wasn't right. Mountain Girl agreed and said, "Let's get out of here."

"It doesn't matter. There's no contract. Fuck it."

Just then we heard over the sound system, "Ladies and gentleman, the greatest rock 'n' roll band in the world—The Rolling Stones."

From the helicopter, the Earth looked gouged out. Seismic faults ruptured the landscape.

Fallen Angels

"Altamont" is synonymous with "disaster," the end of the sixties. One asshole pulled a gun and got killed by a Hell's Angel. Terry the Tramp was the Angel most closely involved with this event and was held responsible by his brother riders for the PR disaster. He took his own life in Bear's house in the Oakland Hills on February 13, 1970. Terry the Tramp was a man of honor, a beautiful person who won my eternal gratitude and affection. I am not alone in that regard.

Down on Bourbon Street

I was sitting in class when it hit me—a horrible cramp in my stomach. I tried to ignore it and it happened again. I turned to my friend, also a hippie and a student, like me, and held my stomach, grimacing. This was no ordinary pain.

"Get me to a doctor," I moaned.

The UC infirmary didn't mess around. They immediately put me on a gurney and wheeled me into an examination room. The obstetrician wore her white hair in a bun like my Grandma Sarah. When she inserted a speculum, I screamed. She said, "You have PID, a sexually transmitted disease that started locally as gonorrhea and ascended into your fallopian tubes. Didn't you notice a smell?"

Free love was fraught with danger. You didn't ask a sexual history. You acted on impulse. You grabbed each other. You tore off your clothes. You hardly ever wore

underwear and never under a long skirt and peasant
blouse. You wanted to be nude. We women around
Berkeley in 1970 were a new breed, free to express our
sexuality and smarts, but there was a price to pay.

"PID. What do the initials mean?" asked my rational mind.

"Pelvic inflammatory disease. You're in the hospital
for a ten-day course of intravenous penicillin. You must
immediately inform your husband."

I looked up, barely able to raise my chest from the
gurney. "Husband? Lovers," I said and passed out.

The next day I dragged the IV pole to the public
telephone near the nurses' station, only slightly more
coherent. I had to reach Bear in New Orleans.

I called the Royal Hotel on Bourbon Street and asked
for Bear. No one was registered under that name, the
receptionist told me.

"Impossible." I cried. "He's there. He's with the
Grateful Dead."

"With the what dead?" I dropped the receiver. A nurse
saw the incident and ran over.

"What are you doing? You are not supposed to be out
of bed," she scolded. There were no phones in hospital
rooms in those days.

The nurse took the receiver, "I'll call for you. Here.
Give me that."

I gave her the Grateful Dead's itinerary, and she dialed
the hotel.

"What's his name?" she asked.

"Owsley Stanley."

"No one is registered under that name, Rhoney. Now get
back in bed."

Even the stiff nurse felt sorry for me. She put her arm
under mine and escorted me back to bed, wheeling the IV

line behind me. Everywhere I moved, I dragged the IV pole. I fell into unconsciousness and woke in the middle of the night. I shuffled out in my hospital slippers to the public telephone and called the hotel again in New Orleans.

The receptionist asked for a name. "Try 'The Bear'!" No answer. "Would you like to try someone else?"

"Try Ramon Rodriques," I said, and Ramrod picked up. "Where's Bear?"

"We got busted," Ramrod replied. "Set up is more like it. He's in jail."

I felt like a punch in the stomach.

"Oh, no," I finally said. "Will they let him out?"

"Al Matthews is working on it. They let the rest of the band out. We have a gig tonight."

I lay in bed watching the penicillin drip into my vein, taking measure of my life. The days passed like weeks, my mind numb from the damage to my body and the IV fix.

Bear visited me in a fox fur coat. He had been on the road to Hawaii and New Orleans, and true, it was winter in California, but this was a fashion statement.

"How could you get busted, Bear? Why did you mess around with underage girls?" I asked rhetorically.

"How come you got the clap, Rhoney?"

"It was a mistake. I guess it could happen to anybody, couldn't it?" I couldn't resist hugging him. I felt sorry for him, but I was mad.

He put his hand under the covers. It had been too long since I had felt desire. The monitor went *beep-beep-beep*, and the nurse rushed in and fixed the IV line.

Bear confided, "The Feds are threatening to rescind my bail. They want me to start serving my sentence now, even before the appeal is decided."

"Well, don't risk getting busted again!" I managed, and fell back on the pillow exhausted.

"I can't stay. We're broadcasting the Grateful Dead live from the Family Dog."

I had been in the hospital for days. I had lost track of time.

Bear handed me a get-well gift in a gift shop bag— *Portnoy's Complaint* by Philip Roth.

"This is a best seller, a Jewish writer, very hot." Bear hadn't even removed his coat and he was gone. When I read the book, it seemed to be about masturbation.

On the tenth day of my tether to the penicillin, I woke up with bulbous knees, swollen lips, itchy skin, and a rash on my body. My face felt taut, as if the blood vessels in my neck were constricting and tightening from below upward.

"Code red!" shouted the nurse, and pulled the IV line out of my arm. She gave me a shot of epinephrine and saved my life. I was covered with welts and swollen, but the doctors assured me this was normal after the adverse reaction.

"Adverse reaction?"

The doctor explained I had an allergic reaction to penicillin."

I wasn't allergic to penicillin before I came to the hospital, and now I was freaked out. Whatever releases they requested, I signed; whatever medicine they gave me, I accepted—a tube of cortisone cream for my welts and pills to take three times a day. At their insistence I made an appointment for liver function tests.

They warned me, "Now you are allergic to penicillin. You must highlight this on any medical record." I didn't even thank them. I fled to Bear's house.

Phil Lesh answered the door.

He put his finger over his lips. "Shh! Bear's on the phone with the lawyers. The Feds are attempting to revoke his right to travel." I followed him upstairs and greeted Bear, who grunted with a shake of his nude butt and turned to the window in a very serious phone conversation.

Phil shook his head with discouragement, walked into the living room, whispering to me, "We have four shows in New York with the Allman Brothers and he . . ." He looked up and pointed to Bear, "he intends to record."

Now I was worried.

I was wearing the same clothes from ten days ago. Time had moved while I was away.

Phil noticed me. "Rhoney, what happened to you? Are you okay?"

I told him my experience.

He brought me a glass of water so I could take the meds. Bear finally got off the phone. He was jumping up and down. The Feds couldn't do it. They couldn't revoke his bail. Their own red tape got in the way. Too much paperwork!

Recovery was slow. Going to UC Berkeley Graduate School took all my energy. I stopped working as Lenny Hart's secretary. When the band was on the road in New York, Mountain Girl invited me over to meet the baby, Annabelle. I was astonished when I saw her. I had envisioned babies more like pinkies, but Annabelle was fully formed—a miniature individual. She hung on Mountain Girl's breast and did not cry when Mountain Girl put her on the floor as long as she had something in her mouth.

"Annabelle Bluebird Gingerbear Garcia. Hunter named her." Mountain Girl changed her cloth diaper using big silver safety pins—a gift from one of Garcia's admirers.

Before 1966, Mountain Girl had been Carolyn Adams of
Hyde Park, New York. Everybody comes from somewhere.

She strapped on a Snugli and held Annabelle close to
her chest, and we walked outside. Their house, which they
shared with Hunter, was in Madrone Canyon, and their
backyard dropped into the woods. Hunter sat on a swing
strung from a great branch of a Madrone tree, his arms
taut around the ropes. I ran over to him just as he leaned
back. He swung high above my head, soared into the sky,
and leaped from the swing to the soft ground below.

I ran down the hill, crying, "Hunter, Hunter, are
you high?" When I reached the bottom of the ravine,
panting and out of breath, he was dusting himself off
and laughing.

He took my hand and pulled me up the hill. He
pointed at the swing. "Get on!" he ordered. His voice was
gruff, not so much from cigarettes as his manner.

I looked down into a deep gully. "I will not." I was afraid.

"You only learn from falling. If you fall, I'll catch you.
If you don't fall, I'll catch you anyway. Come on, Rhoney.
Courage! We're in this together."

I was willing to take a chance. I took a breath, sailed
into the air, and when Hunter said "jump," I jumped.

I fell to the ground, but he was there and he held me. We
rolled down the hill to the bottom together. It was cathartic.

Call it first Saturn returns. Call it an epiphany—the
revelation of my path. Fear was not the silencer. Action
in the face of fear was possible. I had my inspiration
and knew what I wanted. I wanted a child with Bear—
whatever it took.

Papa Bear

Bear and I sat in the kitchen at his place in the Oakland Hills at a table that looked like it came from Sears.

I was in a fertile groove. "How do you feel about children?" I asked him.

"What a silly question. I love children. I have two. You know that. It's only their crazy mothers that kept me away from them. I want more children. I want you and Melissa to have kids."

"Oh, come on, Bear. What happened the last time you called your daughter Nina?"

Bear didn't shirk away. He looked at me.

"She didn't take the call. She won't talk to me. Because I left her with her mother. Because I left."

"Right. And Pete disappeared, too."

Bear had a pained expression. "We discovered too many things missing. He couldn't stay."

I remembered the beaded necklace I had made on a loom, using the pattern of a Navajo design. I sewed the beaded strip to a piece of leather with a special triangular needle. And then it went missing. I couldn't find it. I looked all over. It turned up around Pete's neck and I didn't have the heart to tell him to take it off, that I didn't appreciate that he had taken it without me giving it to him. I made another one in red, white, and blue for myself.

Bear had been an absent father for too long. Pete was already set in his ways when he showed up in Marin. It was too late for Bear to make up the missing time.

"So what makes you think it would be different if Melissa and I had children?"

"You both have taken so many psychedelics, you've raised your consciousness. You can do anything." He chuckled. "These kids will be different. They'll be psychedelic."

I wondered if I could get pregnant, after two abortions and a miscarriage.

Bear nudged at me, pinched my butt, and tweaked my nipples. "Want a quickie?" he whispered.

We all had our wants.

When Sue Swanson's yellow lab, Lady, was having puppies, she said I could have one. "She's not a purebred, but if you want a pup, get on over here. This mama's about to pop."

"Wow. I've never seen puppies born."

"Well, get on over here. That's what I'm telling you. You may want one."

In the background I heard Josh, Rakow and Swanson's boy, screaming.

"I gotta go. Joshua's wet. Wait 'til you have a kid. You won't have time to think of anything but the present."

The day was dry and muggy in Black Point, and the mud was up. The Sacramento River was dried up and looked more like a bog than a body of water—a wetland habitat, not for humans. Kidd was shooting BB's with an air gun into the river. There was a wild cat out there.

He stood up, slanted his head at a target, strained his neck, and aimed. The bullet popped out of the gun, and I watched the cat dart fearfully into the mud.

"Kidd," I screamed, "you almost shot the cat. Are you for real?"

"You know you hate that cat, Rhoney."

"Yeah, but that's no reason to shoot it."

"That's a mean cat, Rhoney. I saw him attack a cock."

I looked askance at him. "A cock? Is that a joke, Kidd?"

"Rhoney, a rooster."

I made a face. "Well, maybe that's the natural order! I don't know. But a cat and a cock fighting is no reason for you to shoot the cat."

"Give me a break. I'm just scaring it."

I couldn't change Kidd. What did I know anyway? We were all just links in the human asshole chain.

"I'm going to Swanson's. Lady's having puppies."

"That's one cool dog."

"Tell Bear if he shows up. Make him wait!" What a joke. I laughed, got into my car, prayed I wouldn't run out of gas, and backed into the dirt road in front of the house.

I bumped along on the rough unpaved road, up the hill, and down to the convenience store, which was closed. "Happy Easter" read the sign on the door. I had no idea. I drove across the railroad tracks onto the high plateau of the Green Point section of Novato. It hadn't rained for weeks and the landscape was dry, littered with strips of eucalyptus bark. It was a quiet Sunday afternoon in March, and I was on a deserted stretch of the service road to California Highway 37.

The car lurched forward, then back, then stopped. I smelled fumes. Bear had taught me that smelling gas was a good sign. It meant there was gas in the lines, and I might be able to get the car going again. He had explained that I had to pump the gas pedal until the coils fired. If I pumped too hard or too long, I could flood the engine and the car wouldn't start, but if I pumped the gas pedal just right, the coils could ignite and fire the engine. There was a fine line, he warned.

Everything with Bear had a fine line. I took a chance. I pumped the gas pedal. What choice did I have?

No sputter. No start. Nothing. My car was out of gas.

I will walk, I decided. I got out of the car, looked up and down the road, but there was nothing—no houses, no stores, no cars, no arbor of trees with shade. I got back in the car and waited. I broke down and cried, no one to witness, no way to go.

For hours I sat there staring off into the distance until finally I heard the whir of an oncoming car and saw the billowing dust of its approach. I leaned on the horn and made a racket.

"Help, help," I shouted, feeling desperate. My voice was hardly loud enough to carry.

The vehicle on the other side of the road stopped and a man with his hands covering his ears approached. When I recognized Bear, I couldn't believe it. How uncanny that he came driving down the road at the exact moment I needed him most. I felt as if the universe wanted us to be together.

"Stop all that racket, Rhoney! What's the matter with you? Do you want me to go deaf?" my guardian angel said.

Feeling like a fool, I admitted I had run out of gas.

"Let's move your car to the side of the road. Get in and release the emergency brake. You steer. I'll push."

When he was satisfied that the car was secure at the side of the road and not a safety hazard, I climbed into his red truck. My heart was beating wildly. I hugged him passionately. He put his hand under my dress. "Why don't we do it in the road?" he said.

"Like George Harrison's monkeys in Rishikesh, India," I responded.

By the time we got to Black Point, we couldn't keep our hands off each other and headed straight for the bedroom.

"You are my Sir Galahad," I told Bear and kissed him. The house was quiet. Kidd was out with the Grateful Dead's equipment. "If you hadn't come along when you did, I don't know what I would have done. You are my hero."

Bear was usually brusque with compliments, but this night, he basked in the attention and pulled me close to him.

"I was desperate. I would have let anyone pick me up, but it was you. You helped me. You came down the road like a vision. I still can't believe it." I felt so tender toward him. The bedroom was our love nest. We watched birds dip into the swampy inlet of the river for food. The light was different. We were past the spring equinox, and the light reflected off the water shimmered. We watched the morning dawn.

Two weeks later, Sue Swanson called. "Too bad. All the pups are gone. You didn't get one."

Two months later, the hospital called. "Your results are back. You're pregnant."

I went to Alembic to talk to Bear. He was in the back, preoccupied with the Grateful Dead's sound equipment.

"I may be going to jail," he conceded. "I must have time to work on the equipment."

I didn't tell him I was pregnant. Instead, I went to Richard Alpert for advice. Our friendship went back to the earliest LSD days, and we were both Jewish. When I first met him, the hair on his head was short and curly, and he had no facial hair. He wore penny loafers or docksides and looked the part of an Ivy League professor. He had long straight legs and danced as if he had training. Since his return from India many people referred to him as "Baba Ram Dass" or "Baba" or "Ram Dass." He was wearing white robes and his beard was getting long. Now

that he was a baba, he looked more like a humble servant
of God dedicated to devotion than a professor, but the
blue eyes and the mischievous twinkle were the same. He
made a gesture with his hands, his long curved fingers
slashing the air.

"I'm pregnant," I told him. "I think it's Bear's kid. I
don't know if I should have it. I don't think Bear will be
there for me."

"He won't," he said. "Even if he says he will, even if
he tells you in detail how to raise this child, he will not
be there for you, be present in the way you and the child
need. Accept it!" He chuckled, rubbed my belly, looked up
to heaven, and sighed.

"So that means I have to make this decision on my own.
If I have the baby, I have to take full responsibility. Fuck."

Richard looked at me sternly. "If you want this baby,
have it yourself. Don't count on Bear. Do what you want."

"I actually got pregnant on Easter Sunday. What if the
baby's born on Christmas?"

Richard laughed. "Won't happen—not to a Jewish
American princess. No chance."

I was in my third month of pregnancy. My due date
was December 23.

I established a morning routine. I got up and made a
drink of blackstrap molasses, wheat germ, and brewer's
yeast. I whirred the blender at the highest speed. I
messed up the kitchen, pouring out the sticky molasses,
supposedly very rich in bioavailable iron. At least it
sweetened the concoction. As far as giving up the hard
drugs—it was easy. Hear less music. Have less sex. Here
I was having a child, and I had never even had a pet. My
mother said animals were dirty and were not allowed in
the house. I was born cross-eyed, and that set up my place

in the family. All of us had been burned by our blood relatives. Our parents' words colored our thoughts, but it was up to us to take that heritage and find right action.

The Caged Bear and Double Mammy

The time came when Bear had to turn himself in to serve
his three-year prison sentence. He had flouted the law
repeatedly and his arrest record was getting larger. After
the big bust in December 1967 came the New Orleans bust
with the Grateful Dead in January 1970. The final blow
was his arrest on July 15 with Betty and Bob Mathews for
possession of marijuana at their home in the Oakland Hills.
At the July 21 hearing for revocation of bail in the United
States District Court, Judge William T. Sweigert fixed bail
at $70,000, a staggering amount for those days. Not only
would Bear have to come up with the cash but also he had
to show assets worth that amount. This he could not do.

"You take the owl," he said. "Melissa has Chopper the
cat, and Screech cannot be around that cat." The owl and
Bear looked at each other, and I was sad.

"Fuck the law," I said. "You don't have to turn yourself
in. You can skip bail and go to Canada, take on a new
identity. We can be free." The Hell's Angels would help
him cross the border. I would join him. The baby could
have dual citizenship.

But Bear did not hear me. He fought long and hard for a
reversal of his sentence, from December 21, 1967, onward
and lost every appeal up through the United States Supreme
Court. When he lost, he accepted that it was his duty as an
American citizen to do time. He refused to run away.

"There was never justice," I exclaimed. "What about
the way the founding fathers treated blacks, as nonpeople?

And women, and even white men who had no property were not allowed to vote."

To Bear, the manufacture of LSD was the right of personal domain and a victimless crime. He believed that the philosophical thought that went into the writing of the Constitution still prevailed and that real change came from within. It was only after he was in prison that his viewpoint changed. It was sad to see him let it go. Prison made him a bona fide outlaw and an enemy of his country.

While he was in the Oakland jail waiting to be moved to federal prison, an inmate broke Bear's nose. He thought he should have plastic surgery, but the staff doctor at the jail literally gave him a Band-Aid.

I was outraged and phoned the Federal Bureau of Prisons, crying, "The father of my unborn child has been attacked by another prisoner!"

I could not even get through to an official in charge who knew about the situation. The official on the phone said, "Listen, lady. There are twenty-five facilities and twenty-five thousand inmates in the federal system. In a city jail, a punch in the nose is routine." I phoned Al Matthews, the lawyer in LA. Melissa asked Jack to use his Jefferson Airplane connections, but to no avail.

Neither Melissa nor I was allowed to visit Bear as we were coconspirators in the original arrest. Some prison regulation, a pretense that prison was rehab and that former cohorts could cause recidivism. I called the lawyer again. I didn't care that phone time was a billable expense. "Is it true that I'm not allowed to visit Bear? He's the father of my child. I'm like . . . his wife."

"That's right," said the lawyer. "Those are the rules."

Distracted with worry, my imagination went wild. I pictured Bear as the victim of random vicious assaults, getting beat up and butt-fucked. Man can grow to tolerate anything. Would Bear become a monster?

Fuck the system, I decided. I borrowed ID from my friend Deb. I looked nothing like her, but at that time IDs had no photos. I went to see Bear at the Oakland jail and got in. The waiting room was crowded with lots of black women and crying babies.

Bear sat behind a partition and we spoke on the well-worn telephone through the dirty glass. He had lost weight, and his formerly Roman nose had a camel hump in it; the patrician quality of his face and demeanor that made you know he was a descendant of the Pilgrims on the Mayflower had been replaced by a furtiveness in his eyes, a bend in his back, and shady speech colored with curse words. He was thin and depressed. I didn't ask him about the conditions. We just talked. Finally, the guard said, "Time's up!"

Bear growled into the phone. "Let Melissa use Deb's ID, and the two of you alternate visiting days."

When I called Melissa to give her an update, she said, "We have no time to visit Bear. We have to move his stuff out of the house. Ramrod has agreed to move the boxes into a garage space in Berkeley, so it's all about packing right now."

When I met Melissa at Bear's house, she was wearing a colorful Guatemalan serape based on traditional Mayan dress, hand-woven heavy cotton in earth pigments, rust and brown, three panels sewn together with a decorative neck design of stylized geometric animals. When I had first seen this outfit on her, I thought it was unsophisticated. Then I saw Jack on stage playing bass with the Jefferson Airplane wearing the male version of the serape, and *I* felt unsophisticated.

Without furniture, the house reminded me it had been the old Ali Akbar Khan School of Music. We packed the books first and then confronted Bear's massive collection of stuff—cables, connectors, batteries, stereo parts, records, tapes, kitchen equipment, contraband paraphernalia. I was daunted by the display while Melissa neatly folded all the clothes.

When the first box filled up, I lifted it and moved it aside. I leaned back against the wall, exhausted. "Melissa," I said. "I should be resting. I'm pregnant. I'm not supposed to lift heavy boxes."

My breasts were sensitive and hurt. The bust of my soft, brushed cotton dress was too tight. Sitting on a box, resting against the wall, I snapped the elastic, pulling the bodice forward.

Melissa laughed. "Rhoney, I don't know how to tell you this, but . . . ." She paused. "I'm pregnant, too."

I fell off my box onto the floor.

Melissa and I alternated visiting Bear in the Oakland Jail, both with Deb's ID, both pregnant. The guards never questioned us. "What will happen when I have the baby?" I asked Bear.

"Don't worry. Telephone me as soon as you have the baby."

On December 21, two days early, I went into labor. My water broke and the contractions came one after another, a wrenching of my insides that never stopped. I had planned a home delivery, but after twenty-four hours of labor, nothing was happening. The midwife decided no home birth for me, that I needed hospital monitoring. This was not what I wanted—vulnerable to judgment, a woman having a baby without a husband, but the safety of the child was paramount, and I was carted to the Petaluma General Hospital in the back of Sue's station wagon.

"Screw this 'baby born at home' shit," she yelled, driving up the dirt road on the way to the hospital.

I moaned, my voice shaking as we went over the bumps. Bear had told me, "You want to have the baby at home, take an apartment next to the hospital." Did I listen? I was relieved when I was the only one in the maternity ward. Melissa showed up and wanted to go into the delivery room, but Sue knew the rules. Only one pregnant person in the delivery room.

"A boy," they shouted out, holding up the baby by his feet so I could see his penis.

I was surprised. Bear said I was having a girl. We had picked out only girl names—Sage, Egret, and Iridesca. The nurses called him "Baby." I was asked what to put on the birth certificate. I needed to talk to Bear.

Days after Christmas in downtown Oakland, a shopper's hellhole—and I was out there in the morning with my black-eyed beauty. Baby's first outing was to the Oakland Jail to meet his daddy and get a name.

When I arrived with the baby wrapped in a yellow blanket, Bear's favorite color, I was the first one in line. A few Hell's Angel chicks showed up, wearing denim miniskirts and motorcycle boots as if their Harley Davidsons were parked outside. My baby slept through visiting room cacophony, strands of black silk baby hair sprouting out of his round little head. At precisely eleven o'clock, the bell sounded, the officer unlocked the visiting room door, and I was the first to enter. Usually there was a throng of women, all rushing to get to the best telephone, the one with the least amount of crackle, but not today. Even security was kind.

I held the baby up to the dirty glass of the partition. I peeled away his blankets so Bear could see his cute little naked body. He still wasn't circumcised. It wasn't eight days yet, and I was following the Jewish tradition, with Ramrod standing in Owsley's stead. No women, just as the custom would have it.

Bear made cartoon faces and cooed at the baby, who tilted back his head, laughing and gurgling. I sat in the wooden seat and picked up the telephone.

"His name came to me a few minutes after the phone call. Starfinder. Now that I see him, I know that's his name. It's a name that has meaning. It's English, the language we speak. Names have power and create images in the minds of those who hear them." Owsley stared intensely at the baby. On the telephone, I was silent.

"Time's up, ma'am. The next person is waiting," a guard reminded me. I turned my head to the hallway where the waiting line formed. A Hell's Angel was restraining a bunch of frustrated women from trampling me on the way to the telephones.

Bear said, "You'd better go now. This is too much for the baby." I looked at Starfinder.

Bear got up. He turned and gave a little wave. His nose was bent and his ass was skinny.

At the next visiting day, a very pregnant "Deb" visited Bear. "I thought you had the baby," an aggressive guard confronted Melissa. She was very distressed. The next time I saw the guard I told him he was hallucinating.

On Saturday, January 16, I left Starfinder with Melissa at her home in San Francisco, for a much needed break. The baby was just over three weeks old, having been born on a Tuesday. Melissa was alone, Jack on the road with the Airplane. When I returned, the door was ajar and I called out, "Melissa." No one answered.

I crept quietly through the house and heard, "In here, Rhoney." I had never been in Jack and Melissa's bedroom.

There was Melissa, spread out on a fur in a king-size bed, Starfinder at her breast. "The baby was crying and I gave him titty. I think I'm in labor." Melissa was looking uncomfortably pregnant. I sat on the bed and tried not to see Jack's doeskin pants flung across the chair.

I went into a long-winded explanation to hide my anxiety at Melissa's condition. "Suckling brings on contractions. That's why it's so good to nurse after delivery. The infant's sucking causes uterine contractions, and necrotic placental and uterine tissue are expelled."

Melissa's belly rose and immediately fell. She writhed on the bed. "How long have you been having contractions?" I asked nonchalantly. "Maybe it's time to go to the hospital."

"No. Jack is not here. I am not due for three weeks," Melissa said, in denial. "This has just started." But in five minutes she had another contraction, and another five minutes later, at which point I announced we were going to the hospital.

"No," she calmly declared, "you take care of Starfinder." She called Ron Wickersham's wife, who was at the house in five minutes, with a blanket in the back of her station wagon. I strapped Starfinder into his car seat and followed them to the San Francisco Hospital.

I paced outside with the baby at my breast. Melissa screamed many times before her baby popped out.

Jack came back from the road and took no visitors. Bear sent word through the Hell's Angels that Melissa's baby's name was Iridesca. Jack did not like it.

Bear was transferred to Terminal Island Prison, the notorious Federal Correctional Institution south of Los Angeles. I drove from Marin in my blue Mercedes,

Starfinder strapped in the back. Terminal Island Prison was next to a naval base and surrounded by a high wire fence. Armed guards watched from towers. There were more guards than people. At the first gate, a uniform curtly demanded my ID. The baby was in a Snugli close to my chest, and the guard didn't smile. Controlling my authority issues, I handed the officer the Pennsylvania driver's license belonging to Deb. He checked the list of visitors; I signed the "Notification to Visitor" form. *Clang* went the metal gate as it rose. *Clang, clang* behind me.

My heart was racing. The baby kicked at me, sensing my fear. I stopped at the next checkpoint. Another guard perched on a stool wanted my ID. We were led to a room where Bear was hunched in a chair, wearing a buttoned khaki shirt, pants with a military-looking canvas belt, and leather shoes.

Bear said, "I am only allowed to embrace you now and at the end." I handed him the baby. He whispered to me, "I hate this place. Most of the guards here are military." He touched his nose. "It's lucky I started in Oakland. If I had come here raw, I wouldn't have made it. I've applied for a transfer. This prison is for felons. I'm charged with a misdemeanor. I really don't belong here. They all know it." The baby gurgled and Bear laughed.

The thin guard came over, bent down to my ear, and told me it was time to leave. He had actually given us more time than was permitted. Bear pushed his chair away from the table and handed me the baby. The scraping on the floor echoed in the empty room. He kissed me and gave the baby a tummy squeeze. Another guard appeared. One in front, one behind, they marched straight ahead through the thick metal door. Bear turned his head. "This sucks," he mouthed. Starfinder was crying for breast milk as we ran from the room. At each checkpoint I was forced to produce my ID to exit the prison. As the last gate lifted, I rushed to the parking lot and whipped out my breast. The warm, sweet milk was dribbling out. Bear had said to only feed the baby mother's milk. Starfinder cooed.

The Grateful Dead performed at Terminal Island Prison, August 4, 1971. Bear was given free range and introduced us to a new friend, a hardened felon who helped him set up the stage and the sound for the show. Melissa and I brought the babies, but they were too cranky for us to stay. Bear kissed us good-bye. He was being moved to Lompoc Correctional Complex, the so-called "country club" of federal prisons.

"Contact Ginger and Shuster," he advised. "They live near Lompoc. If you stay with them, you could come everyday. Bring the baby."

Lompoc is twenty miles from the Pacific Ocean, in the Santa Ynez Valley, surrounded by mountains. Bear had permission to see his visitors outdoors for a picnic. Melissa borrowed Jack's Citroën sedan, and we headed for Santa Barbara with the kids on a beautiful day. The babies were restless, swatting at each other and shrieking shrill sounds.

"Quiet down!" Melissa commanded, "I can't drive with that screeching."

"They're just kids," I yelled at her. "You don't have to be the one in control." Suddenly, she stopped the car and slapped Starfinder on the head. He and Iridesca were immediately silent. Angry, I pushed open the door. Then the babies both started crying. Holy moly. Melissa had driven off the road so the car was literally at a tilt.

I opened the back door. The babies were holding hands. "Rhoney, I'm really sorry. I apologize." Melissa began. She glared at me and spoke in even, placating tones. "Jack wants her named Redbird and I agreed. Today I am telling Bear."

The babies' faces lolled to the side. Finally they looked like they were asleep. I patted them on their heads. Starfinder had soft blonde curls but Redbird was bald. Jack had followed a Chinese tradition of shaving a baby's head to make the hair grow back thicker. I got into the passenger seat. Melissa turned on the engine, the Citroën levitated, then purred, and dropped onto the road. We drove in silence on a ridge along the Pacific. The sky looked very close and blue, luminous from the reflection of the ocean. We saw the Federal Correctional Institution signs and drove through rolling hills and eucalyptus groves to the parking lot. Lompoc, we were informed by a pleasant guard, had no walls, fences, bars, gun towers, or guns. There were flower gardens. What a difference from Terminal Island.

With the babies strapped to our bellies in their Snuglis, carrying picnic baskets, we joined other women with their baskets and kids and walked across the parking lot to the prison. I could see Bear sitting with other plainly dressed inmates on plastic lawn chairs. His hair was short and buzzed. We walked around a lawn fence, and the five of us hugged.

We spread a checkered tablecloth on the ground. Melissa whispered to Bear, bending down low, but I could hear. Bear was silent, then said, "Redbird, from Native American folklore and the Charlie Parker tune. . . . I like!" Bear smiled, held up the baby, "Redbird," he boasted to his buddies. Bear and his buddies chowed on chicken, cheese, nuts, and blueberries, and Melissa and I breast-fed the babies.

On the way back, Melissa apologized again for slapping Starfinder, but I couldn't get it out of my mind. What was right action?

I decided that one year in one home was a good start for my son, but after that it was the road. I gave up my home in Black Point and stayed with friends. We visited Bear at every opportunity. I followed his diet for Starfinder and only gave him breast milk and meat. As I was breast-feeding that meant I ate the same way.

Bear said, "Don't give him Zwieback crackers for teething. Make beef jerky."

Before I headed for Lompoc, I used The New Riders' kitchen at Kentfield to make beef jerky. First I bought velvet steak with no fat, thinly sliced by the butcher, which I cut into strips and marinated without salt, according to Bear's recipe. The meat dried on the racks in the oven at a very low temperature with the oven door slightly open for bursts of time. Making beef jerky was no easy task, but we all felt sorry that Bear was in jail, and nobody complained. I made marijuana butter according to Mountain Girl's recipe. The kitchen was a mess with dripped butter on the stove and running down the counters. Everyone complained.

I left early—Highway 101 to Gilroy to 1. Daily count was at four o'clock, but on weekends, inmates stood by their beds to be counted at ten o'clock in the morning, no talking, no moving. I wanted to be there on time.

We went to a fenced-in patio seating area. Bear brought out a leather pouch tied with a colorful string. He unwound the string, opened the bag, and showed me a piece of jewelry, a heavy metal heart with wings running through it on a leather thong. He pulled a polishing cloth out of his pocket, gave it a final buff, and hung it around my neck. "I'm working in the shop, learning metallurgy, making jewelry. This is for you." He turned me around and tied the piece around my neck. "It doesn't lie exactly flat. My first piece. I'll get better."

The baby hung on to Bear's pants to pull himself upright. "Hey, Bear, look, Starfinder is standing."

"Rhoney, he's not standing, he's walking." Our son was wearing a deerskin shirt with turquoise beads from one of Bear's friends, his blonde hair curled at the ends. Bear was joyful. Starfinder toppled over and howled. I shoved titty in his mouth, and he sucked contentedly.

Bear told me about prison life. He had been assigned to the laundry, and this gave him a lot of perks which he used mainly to support his carnivorous diet. Then he was put in charge of the gym. "I've been working out. That's one thing I can do in here. I'm getting the equipment in order and purchasing new weights. Their setup is very antiquated." He rippled his biceps. The muscle popped right out of his shirt and it was huge. He flexed his arm. "Feel my muscle," he ordered.

I put the baby in his little carrier and we dry fucked to the best of our ability.

Release

Melissa and I had the discussion. She wanted to be the one
to pick up Bear when he got out of prison; so did I. In the
beginning, we agreed to alternate visiting days. In reality,
she was much too busy and rarely visited. We looked at
the calendar and calculated alternate weeks, and Saturday
morning, July 15, 1972, was my turn to visit. Bear had
served more than two years consecutively in federal prisons
and had done the rest of the time in local prisons during his
long appeal.

Would Bear walk out through the prison gate and look for
me or Melissa?

When I pulled up, he was sitting on a bench outside
the wall with a large duffel bag waiting for me. I was late.
Before I could open the car door, he had thrown the bag
next to the baby. "The car looks good." I had washed and
cleaned his precious Mercedes 190, a royal blue four-door
sedan. The baby and I had been practically living out of it
to visit Bear at Lompoc. He smiled. "Move over." He took
the wheel, and we headed north.

I looked at Bear's face in the light of day. He looked older.
The lines in his forehead were deep and grooved. Why hadn't
I noticed this on my visits?

I had made lunch reservations at The Nepenthe in
Big Sur, an expensive restaurant overlooking the Pacific.
I could afford it; the Grateful Dead had paid me a salary
while Bear was incarcerated. We walked up the steep
stone stairs and headed for a table on the verandah. There

were photos of famous patrons including Rita Hayworth and Orson Welles. Bear was unsteady and demanded my full attention. At a round table next to the cliff, a bunch of rowdy friends in tight jeans, tie-dyes, and sandals were making a lot of noise. One of them recognized Owsley. So soon out of jail, Owsley felt as if they were paparazzi and he was a celebrity. We made a fast getaway. We left without eating and jumped back onto the highway.

I haltingly told him I had fantasized about making love on the beach. He said, "Don't you remember how sand is not fucking friendly?" It took me a minute to get the joke. The homecoming was not going well.

I had rented a house in Berkeley for the week. It was furnished, but there was no food in the refrigerator. "Not to worry," I said, "Starfinder and I will go to the supermarket and we'll be right back." When we got back from the store with the bacon, eggs, steak, cream, and butter, he was gone.

As a more permanent home, I had leased a house in Stinson Beach for Bear, Starfinder, and me, but this was a big mistake. True, the house was on the hill overlooking the Pacific Ocean, down the street from Mountain Girl and Garcia, Muir Woods the backyard, but how was the King of LSD going to make the drive home every night over fogged-in Mt. Tamalpais or around the winding foggy coast road? Obviously, Bear didn't. He stayed in town. The house in Stinson had a child's room with a crib in it and a master bedroom for the child's parents, but this scenario, my dream of a family, was not happening. I listened to the ocean waves roll on the beach and recede, tuning in to the rhythm to clear my mind. In an empty field, seeds can grow. An even beat gets interrupted.

One of Garcia's neighbors down at the beach knew this girl who was giving aura readings, $50 an hour. I met her at a metaphysical bookstore in San Francisco. She was in a dark back room with a velvet curtain over the window, wearing a colorful gypsy skirt, feathers in her long brown hair. She looked like a hippie. No cards, no crystal ball, she asked me to stand and circled her hands over my head. When she did this, I felt surges of energy. She told me my aura was imbalanced—strong on the mental, spiritual, and psychic levels, but diminished on the material. "Extremely weak," she said, "you need work on the 'material' level."

I was so shocked, believing almost the polar opposite about myself. I listened to the seer, moved to a cheap studio apartment in San Francisco, and enrolled in a five-unit course at San Francisco State in the Zoology Department. Tuition was free for California residents. My class began at eight o'clock in the morning and got me back into school full time. There were field labs to ocean coves to collect specimens, which Starfinder, a precocious toddler, loved, and table labs to tag the specimens with their Greek or Latin identification. I had beautiful handwriting and the professor commended my labels.

The Grateful Dead were playing at Kezar Stadium, trying out Bear's new sound system. I went to the show and brought my text books. I was learning the Linnaen taxonomy, the principles of scientific classification— kingdom, phylum, class, order, family, genus, species. Starfinder followed Bear around the stage, and I found an out of the way spot on the stage to study during the breaks.

Garcia sat on a box at the side of the stage and strummed an unplugged guitar. He was curious about my book and my dedication to studying. I told him my plan of going for a career in science. I was giving up the psychic voodoo for the real stuff. He liked it and encouraged me. I continued with my plan, "I won't have to ask Bear for money. I'll be able to feed my own kid." It was so public asking Bear for money. He would meet me on stage during a show, peel out hundred-dollar bills and make me dance for them.

When I got an A in Zoology, I gained enough confidence to believe that I could succeed and enrolled in a community college to take the basic requirements—inorganic chemistry, biology, and physics—for admission to a professional program in science.

Achieving high grades had never been my goal in school but it sure was now. I had no interest in understanding; I only wanted the highest grade in the class. When I became my physics professor's secretary, my schedule changed. Because of my babysitting issues, Starfinder came with me to college. Bear wanted more time with us, but I was unwilling to accommodate his schedule. Even more than before prison, it was his way or the highway. I did not want confrontation. I had changed my diet to raw carrots and ate nothing else.

One night he called and wanted to visit. I said no. The semester was ending. I was studying. I told him, "Don't come over."

He came and rang the bell downstairs at our apartment on Clement Street for two hours. I did not let him in, gritted my teeth, and studied while he rang the bell. When the grades came out, I had achieved the highest mark in every subject. With a BA from UC Berkeley, basic science credits from San Francisco State and Skyline College, and better than a 4.0 GPA, I was guaranteed acceptance into the dental school of my choice. Tuned into the flow, I decided to go East for school, where no sex, drugs, or rock 'n' roll could distract me from my studies. I started packing for New York.

Strange Love

People change their names for whatever reason. Bear had always hated his long name, Augustus Owsley Stanley III. The concept of being a third was anathema to him. He had suffered through high school with the indignity of Gus. So when he got his prison sentence he took the opportunity to legally change his name from Augustus Owsley Stanley III to Owsley Stanley.

When I decided to go to dental school, I changed my last name to Stanley to match my son's. My profession of dentistry was very conservative, and every day I either wore scrubs or a business suit. Of course, there was the irony. Bear never said anything; whether he knew from irony was another question. There was nothing undesirable about the name Gissen, but I liked the anonymity of Dr. Stanley. Open wide, please.

It was very important to me that Starfinder and Bear have an ongoing relationship. I never took Bear to court for child support. In the summers, I sent Starfinder to be with him in California. I put him on a plane in New York with the arrangement that Bear would meet him in San Francisco. One time I was called by the airline in San Francisco and told nobody was there to pick up my child. "Just wait," I explained. "His father will come." He did. He was late.

Another time I called, Bear picked up, we chatted, and when I asked to speak to Starfinder, he said he wasn't there. "Where is he?" I asked. Bear had sent him to sleepaway camp without telling me. I was pissed. "I send him out to be with you, and you send him away." He was at Wavy Gravy's Camp Winnarainbow and having the time of his life, learning how to juggle, how to walk the tightrope, and taking guitar lessons. During another visit, I phoned, Bear and Starfinder were in Red Rocks on tour with the Grateful Dead. The Grateful Dead were fast becoming the highest grossing touring band in the United States, and Bear was their soundman, building the Wall of Sound and recording every show for his sonic journal.

By the early 1980s, Bear had been fired, but he still went on tour with the Grateful Dead, wearing his laminated all-access pass around his neck and escorting guests backstage, but he used his own money for traveling expenses and had nothing to do with Grateful Dead sound. The metallurgy he had learned in prison became his domain. He sold his art at the Green Peace table during the show. He priced his pieces high. As former King of LSD and innovator of the Wall of Sound, his name alone had value. Deadheads danced through the corridors, high on the music and whatever, especially during Drums, when the guitars left the stage. They were thrilled to meet Owsley and buy his art. His most popular item was a heavy metal belt buckle with a skull and lightning bolt, his iconic symbol of the Grateful Dead that he stenciled in red, white, and blue on the amplifiers before Woodstock to identify Grateful Dead equipment.

Whenever Bear was in New York, Starfinder and I would get together with him, usually at the show or the hotel, but in the fall of 1982, Starfinder, almost twelve, had just started a new school and had too much homework to stay out late. I was getting calls from the teacher every day. I asked Bear if we could agree to meet early. It was hard for us to agree about anything. Neither of us was agreeable by nature. Bear thought this was due to our position in the family. Both of us were older siblings of brothers, domineering and demanding. Bear said your place in the family hierarchy determined your social behavior. Ironically, we agreed about this.

Starfinder and I arrived at Gallagher's, a steakhouse in midtown Manhattan that had sides of beef hanging in the window. The restaurant was empty, but it was early. We took seats at a small table near the bar to wait for Bear. Starf was bent over his sketchpad and I had a book. I had read Bear the riot act on the telephone. "If you're late, I won't wait. If you want to see your kid, be on time."

He said, "If you have to wait for me, the fact that you have a kid will make you more attractive." Huh?

Bear arrived only fifteen minutes late, wearing tight jeans, Tony Lama boots, and a white T-shirt a size too small for his bulging pecs. He had with him a skinny girl who said she was an artist from New Orleans. Starfinder was sketching from a photograph of a wolf. She noticed and showed Bear. "He's good at drawing. He copies well," Bear commented. We all thumbed through Starf's sketchpad. Bear took a case out of his aluminum briefcase, and opened it on the table. It was lined in velvet and contained several pieces of enameled jewelry he had made.

"This is called 'Dark Star.'" He held a jeweler's loupe under my eye so I could see the ornate detail. Another piece was even more gorgeous—a Pegasus enameled in white with tiny rubies in the wings.

"I love it," I said. Bear told me he wanted $10,000, the family price. I was shocked that he wanted me to buy it.

"You're a dentist. You can afford it." The bloody-rare steaks arrived just in time. Bear started eating before his girlfriend's plate was on the table.

"So when are you leaving for Australia?"

He shrugged his shoulders. "In about a month. Why don't you come with us? The big storm is coming, and living in the Northern Hemisphere will be risky." He pointed to Starfinder. "It's obvious he's a natural artist. I can teach him."

He explained how the conditions for the storm were becoming evident. "Near perihelion, the Earth's closest approach to the sun, during a state of low glaciation as measured during an interglacial period, around the winter solstice, the transfer of heat between the equator and the polar regions will be the greatest. When the stored energy reaches a critical stage, one of the normally present Arctic cold-core cyclones will accelerate until it completely takes over the circulation of the Northern Hemisphere. The conditions will resemble those described in the biblical tale of Noah's flood. The disruptive effects will be felt everywhere on the planet. It is doubtful if it is possible to survive this event within the flux area of the storm. We must be in Australia before the winter solstice. We're not going to the coastal regions. We're going up high."

He nudged me in the ribs. "I want you and Starf to come with us." I was threatened by his proposal. I didn't want to lose my son. I put him off by telling him I'd think about it. Better to stay cool, let this be an ordinary time— just two parents meeting to talk about their kid.

A month later Owsley left for Australia, or Oz, as he called it, on a tourist visa. The chick from Gallagher's became his girlfriend in Australia until she got dumped a year or so later.

The terrible twos were nothing compared to the terrible teens. At fifteen, Starfinder ran away from home. For more than a week I did not know where he was. I was hysterical and couldn't sleep. When I did, my nightmares had maimings on country roads and desolate bus stations with phantom shadows. I left an embarrassing message on the answering machine. "Starfinder, if this is you, I love you. I'm sorry for whatever I did. Please let me know your whereabouts." Finally, he called. He was with Bear in California. Bear was living on a monthly basis at the Panama Hotel in San Rafael waiting for his visa to return to Australia. He had sent Starfinder the airplane ticket. I took the next plane to San Francisco. When I saw my son, I burst into tears. He looked ill. His neck was swollen; his voice was a whisper. I was so determined not to react as my mother would that my voice was never louder than my child's. This was not about her and me. This was about Starfinder.

The next day Starfinder decided he would come back with me to New York. By then he had no voice. His neck was so thick, he looked like a Sumo wrestler. The pediatrician in New York diagnosed him with a severe case of mononucleosis and prescribed steroids. I did not fill the doctor's prescription but chose Bear's advice and went to the butcher and bought calves liver, cooked it very rare, and fed it to Starfinder. I kept him in bed for five days. On Saturday, I drove him to school for the College Boards PSAT test, picked him up, fed him more liver, and put him back to bed. When I learned he got a perfect score, I was a doting Jewish mother. By the next week, Starfinder was fully recovered.

Owsley's tourist visa required that he leave Australia every three months. The authorities also became suspicious at the enormous amounts of stuff that Owsley brought into the country. He hired a specialist in immigration to intercede with the officials for him and spared no money to apply for a permanent visa. Finally, his permanent visa was granted, and Owsley settled in

Australia at the mouth of the Walsh River in the middle of nowhere. He lived off the grid. He filtered river water for drinking and collected rain water for other needs. He used generators and windmills for electricity. He squatted on this land he chose, preserving his aversion to ownership. Australia allowed ninety-nine-year leases for squatters. Melissa and her new husband, Jerry Jeffress, bought land upriver to build their own place.

Every January Bear held a Capricorn party at his compound in Australia. The first time I went, I stayed at Melissa's house. On my arrival, we both cried. There had been a lot of water under the bridge, and our friendship had survived. We put love first and made sure our children grew up together. We walked together each morning of my visit. Melissa's legs were strong from climbing up and down the rocky ledges of the Walsh River, following her lanky husband.

Jerry was a bit of a know-it-all, but he really did know it all. He won Oscars for his special effects on *Indiana Jones* and *Star Wars*. His exposition on the flora and fauna of the local landscape was fascinating. He pointed out the varieties of plants and trees that flourished on their homestead. Queensland had the most diverse array of native plants of any state in Australia or in the world. He showed me pink gum trees, conifers, ferns, liverworts, lichens, and wild orchids. Melissa cut in. "Bear's raising orchids at Camp Joule." She liked to call Bear's compound by the original name he gave it and then disclaimed.

I learned to say *Melaleuca quinquenervia*: this is a tree with black bark, the "tea tree" of Australia. We got back to the house right before high noon when the sun was too hot, and the indoors was most welcome. Melissa and I worked at a table loom weaving from yarn she had spun and dyed.

"Why don't you help me with my book?" I said.

She replied, "Oh, God, no. I don't want to recall the little that I think I remember."

As we walked out to watch the sunset, we were contented by the life of our friendship.

The next day was the Capricorn party. A hundred friends from all over the world converged on Bear's compound in the Bush, camping out or staying in tents. My tent had a double bed, Oriental rugs, a cupboard, and a table in the corner for candles.

Bear set up a stage and sound system and arranged for local musicians to perform. Sam Cutler, who was living in Brisbane, brought the band he was managing. Meyer Sound from San Francisco sent a technician. Melissa and Jerry worked the lights and used their video camera to record the show, but they left halfway through because they didn't take the acid Melissa had helped to make thirty years before. They were sleepy and had to go to bed. In the dark, high on LSD, the stars so close at this spot near the equator, no electricity, a flashlight to find my way, I stumbled down a path in the Australian bush, searching for my tent and when I finally found it, I was very happy.

In the morning we gathered in Bear's kitchen for Mean Bean Bear Brew. Bear had planted his own coffee bushes and harvested the beans. He roasted these in a professional roaster. The aroma was so fragrant, I almost did not need coffee, but the coffee he made with real cream was delicious. He used an expensive stainless steel and copper espresso machine, powered by a generator and a stove that was both wood-burning and gas. When the big storm came, we would still have really good coffee.

As Above, So Below

In 2004, Starf, already a veterinarian, and I visited again in
Australia. We were standing in the kitchen when Bear said,
"Feel this." He lifted his son's hand and placed it under his
left jaw. Then it was my turn. It was a hard indurated growth,
only on the left side. Unilateral is a red flag. Not good. Bear
then told us the lump had appeared several months earlier,
and he assumed it was inflammation from a toothache.
None of the doctors saw the integrative approach—that
toothaches can be related to organ systems through the
acupuncture meridians and that a toothache could be a sign
of systemic disease. The dentist extracted the tooth and put
him on antibiotics, but the lump remained, as it did after
the second round of antibiotics. The jaw is avascular, so it
is not unusual for infections in the jaw to take a long time
to heal and to require several courses of antibiotics. When
the lump began to infringe on the recurrent laryngeal nerve
and cause difficulty swallowing, Bear realized this was no
toothache. He went to a local MD who specialized in diseases
of the ear, nose, and throat. The next week, Bear traveled to
the hospital in Cairns for a biopsy: Stage IV squamous cell
carcinoma of the tonsil. Seven months had passed. Radiation
treatment began immediately a three-hour plane ride away,
in Sydney, no surgery. In the United States, surgery is the
treatment of choice for this type of cancer. Bear's doctor
said the treatment with surgery or with chemo or radiation
showed no difference in outcomes. But Bear later believed
the doctor had woefully overestimated the exposure radius
and increased the units of rads, or radiation absorbed doses,
he received and burned him unnecessarily.

He spent three months in Sydney getting treatment.
Starfinder took a month off from his work as a relief

veterinarian and stayed with Bear in Sydney. Redbird
stepped up her wedding date. We all gathered in Cairns
for her wedding on August 20, 2005. Starfinder was the
master of ceremonies, and a very gaunt Bear walked
Redbird down the aisle.

He was still losing weight. He coughed up huge chunks
of yellow phlegm that challenged any social etiquette.
"Don't you think you ought to be more careful? If your
cancer is viral, the virus could be communicable," I
said. He ignored me. Years of frustration challenged
me to my limit. I found myself getting into arguments
with strangers. I argued with Melissa's neighbor about
the training at Australian medical schools and rapped
angrily about how early specialization deprived students
of a liberal arts education and made them mediocre at
diagnosis. He was insulted and told me to go back to the
United States. Aussie men were much too macho for me,
and I took his advice.

When Owsley and Sheilah, his wife, came to New
York City as part of a first-class tour around the world
representing Meyer Sound, I invited them to stay in my
apartment. Owsley's voice was muffled and labored. His
neck had constricting scar tissue, so his posture looked like
he was passing out when he was hacking, heffing, clearing
his throat, and coughing up mucous. When he ate, phlegm
came out of his nose. His table manners weren't so good
to begin with.

He had developed a theory that his cancer came
from the human papilloma virus—warts—and that he
got it from munching on a girl he had met at Kesey's.
"She was all clumpy. I think she had HPV and gave it
to me. I burned warts off my dick so I wouldn't spread
it. The theory of viral cancers," Bear continued, "is not

that the virus causes the cancer but that the virus creates
cell mutations and the mutations generate the cancer.
An oncogene, a cancer-causing gene, can be produced
by the cell. A virus can make an oncogene. DNA can
mutate due to a viral insert. Transcription errors can
cause mutations: a cell replicates itself and makes a
copy of its DNA and fails to copy itself correctly. You
were lucky, Rhoney. Ya know, HPV causes clostridia and
cervical cancer. Now there's a vaccine against the virus,
but the policy is all wrong."

As someone with a master's degree in public health, I
answered Bear, "The Brady Proposal in front of Congress
mandates that all girls must have been vaccinated against
HPV in order to get into public school."

He cut me off. "The boys should be vaccinated, too."

Wow, I thought, he acknowledged sexual equality. We
were agreeing. How nice!

He wandered around my New York City apartment,
looking at my possessions packed up for my move to
Woodstock. My framed posters were wrapped, leaning
against the kitchen wall. Bear absentmindedly popped the
bubble wrap. When he saw one poster, his eyes widened;
he tore off the wrapping and held it up for me to see. It
featured a photo of a nude chick in lotus position.

"That's her. She's the one who got us busted. I told
Spires not to have anything to do with her. He didn't
listen. She introduced him to the narc that got us."

An Anthem for the Bear

Satisfied at whatever comes by its own accord, tolerant of dualities, devoid of envy of others and while performing is equipoised in success or failure is never affected.

By holding on to a dream, never facing reality, subdued colors fade into forms and spices entice householders to make offerings.

Shyamdas   —Bhagavad Gita 4:22

A row of dark-skinned, skinny men, many with turbans, held signs of the names of their arriving passengers at the New Delhi Airport in March 2011. I saw "Dr. Rhoneyji," the tag Shyamdas, my host in India, and I had agreed upon for my sign. I followed the young Indian driver to his car. He spoke no English; I, no Hindi. "Dr.Rhoneyji" and "Shyamdas"—the only words we had in common.

Shyamdas was born in Connecticut as Stephen Schaffer, named by his mother, Gloria, Secretary of State of Connecticut in the 1970s, and his father, Eugene. After he turned eighteen, he moved to India, to the Vrindavan area, where Krishna was born, on the banks of the Yamuna River, a sacred river running parallel to the holy Ganges. Later he divided his time between India and the United States, interpreting the Bhagavad Gita, leading *kirtan* in the tradition of the Braj singers, translating Vedanta from the

Sanskrit. It was he who corrected my Maharishi mantra, not "she-om" but *sri*-om—the goddess of wealth and beauty. Shyamdas had written and published about a dozen books, translations of the Sanskrit scriptures and the local dialects of the fifteenth- and sixteenth-century devotional poets of Braj who lived then where he lived now, by the Govardhan Hill in the Vrindavan area. He also had another apartment in Gokul, the childhood home of Krishna, but we were going to Govardhan Hill. My mission in India was heart opening and joy and connection—a bit corny for someone with my LSD experience.

Govardhan Hill was a three-hour drive from the airport on unpaved one-lane roads, through crowded streets with people pushing past the cars and buggies to shop for food in the roadside markets. My driver inched forward, honking his horn. The car in front honked back. All the drivers were honking. So this is how it goes, I thought, as I rolled up my window. We lunged forward. The driver was on the right, English fashion, and I sat opposite so I could see him. He was unfazed by the noise and traffic and peoples' faces everywhere. I was delighted.

I opened the Hindi app on my iPhone. "Aur kitnee door hai?" the audio teacher sang and I repeated in singsong Hindi.

I translated, imitating the lilt of the voice, "How much further?" Both the driver and I laughed. Then he answered me in Hindi, and I couldn't understand a word. He laughed.

Govardhan Hill—"where cows flourish"—is a legend. According to Hindu folklore, the vengeful deity Indra unleashed rain, lightning, and floods on the people of Braj, but for seven days, Krishna, with his little finger, held up the Govardhan Hill like an umbrella and sheltered the people and the land from the curse of Indra. Every day, hundreds of pilgrims circle fourteen miles around the hill to be closer to Krishna. Some prostrate their bodies, lying flat on their stomachs in the sandstone, get up, put their toes where their heads were, and prostrate again. These devotees spend a month circumambulating the sacred hill.

We drove through rural Indian countryside and finally reached the holy ground of Jatipura, on the southwest side of Govardhan Hill. Up the village road to the end, the driver honking at the sacred cows, around a bend, down another dirt road, and we stopped. A hole in a metal wall was the entrance to Shyamdas's place.

Downstairs was a shop baking flatbread for the temple. Upstairs Shyam was in the middle of his puja, the curtains drawn. Chanting and drumming, harmonium sounds seeped through. At the end he pushed the curtain aside and we all joined in singing Govinda. I moved my body in time to the lilting rhythm. Mohan, Shyam's manservant and brother in devotion to Krishna, prepared lunch for all of us. We sat on rugs; I leaned against the wall. He placed flat grass mats for plates on the floor. From his fist he placed a mound of food on each mat—a green lump, an orange one. He put down another variety, then a third. Next came sweets. All this food had been offered first to Krishna.

Monday morning, I was sitting on the covered porch at Shyam's, adjacent to the monkey bars, watching the monkeys clamber over the thick metal grates, their curved nails hanging on to the metal rods, their tails sweeping the concrete roof, seldom discouraged in their mischief. "Watch out for your glasses," Shyam warned me the first day. "They'll grab them."

Five days later, I still had my glasses. We were leaving Jatipura for our trip to Rajasthan, the land of kings, taking

an overnight train to Nathdwara, the temple of Lord
Shrinathji, the black image of Lord Krishna as a child. In
preparation I was reading Shyam's translation: *Ocean of
Grace: The Teachings of His Holiness Goswami Shri Prathameshji*:
"Everything is Krishna and nothing but Krishna, and . . .
Krishna has two powers: one of action and the other of
knowledge. The Supreme is neither dual nor non-dual.
One without a second."

My head bent around the words. Shyam lectured about
devotion, the Bhakti philosophy—every act performed
with devotion. One achieves enlightenment to open the
heart to love. Enlightenment is a step on the way to love.

My cell phone rang. It was Starfinder. My son was
in Australia with his wife and baby visiting his father,
to introduce Juniper, one year old, to Bear. I said,
"Starfinder, I'm so glad you called." I was so excited to
hear from him, I couldn't stop talking, but he cut me off
asking me where I was, who I was with, and what I was
doing. "Why?" I asked, now worried, hearing something I
had previously missed in his voice.

"MOM, we're all right, but Bear died in a car crash."

I screamed and Shyam ran to me and continued the
conversation with Starfinder. There had been a freak
storm Saturday night, when Bear was driving home to
the Tableland from the airport in Cairns, with his wife,
Sheilah, in the passenger seat. The SUV spun out of
control, went off the road, and hit a grove of trees. Bear
died instantly, and Sheilah fractured her shoulder. "Take
your time, Mom," he said when I got back on the phone,
"we're all moving very slowly."

As soon as I hung up the phone, I knew I must leave
immediately for Australia. Reinforcing my decision,
Shyamdas told me that in Hindu mourning tradition for

thirteen days, the relations of the deceased, dressed in white, the color of purity, were forbidden to enter a Hindu temple and recite sacred texts and perform any Hindu rituals. "Hello?" I said. "Why did I come to India. It wasn't to wear white in March." With great difficulty, we accomplished the paperwork and booked a departure flight to Australia: Jatipura to New Delhi to Bangkok to Brisbane to Cairns.

Starfinder and Cameron, Redbird's husband, picked me up at the airport. No plans, nothing. Nobody wanted to go past the scene of the car accident, and that was the only road home. I rented a suite at a beach hotel in Cairns, and we brought the babies to the beach. Redbird's twins were five months younger than Starfinder's daughter. Sitting in the sun, watching the ocean waves, playing with Phoenix, Gryphon, and Juniper, we slowly healed. More than a week later, we were ready to head up to the Tableland. At the last minute, Redbird, Cameron, and the boys opted not to caravan with us, and we set out in an eight-passenger all-wheel-drive vehicle, Starfinder driving. It was night when we passed the grove of trees where Bear went off the road.

Starfinder naturally assumed responsibility and considered everyone's needs with good sense. He had gotten Bear's personal stuff from the coroner's office and hid his bloodstained jacket from Sheilah. He wore the stealie buckle and the leather belt Bear had made himself in jail. In cases of accident victims, autopsy is generally the rule. No one in the family wanted an autopsy, and Starfinder convinced the coroner to waive it.

Five of us were staying at Bear's compound, including the baby, Juniper. Bear had bought her a playpen, and we set it up in the main shed just past the dining table near the couch. She liked standing in it and gripping the bars.

Slowly, Sheilah chose a day for the funeral, Starfinder supporting her every decision. They chose a time when West Coast friends would be available to Skype, tuning in via computer, Tuesday, March 22, 2011. Sam Cutler arrived from Sydney. The first to release notice to the press of Owsley's death, he was the family's liaison with the media. He ran around committed to setting up the computer for Skype and was generally helpful.

I wrote out a speech to recite at the memorial and read part of it to Starfinder: "Bear was a man who walked his talk, who challenged the cult of personality and wanted the attention of others to focus on his work with sound, his art, and his philosophy, not on him."

Starfinder said, "Mom, what's the point?"

I decided not to speak. Melissa, with no hesitation, declined to speak.

We were late getting to the funeral home on the day of the memorial, Starfinder driving, Sheilah next to him with her shoulder in a sling. We joked about lateness. So like Bear. Nina, his older daughter from his second marriage, sat in the back, pensive. She knew so little about Bear. She didn't even know he was her father until she was fifteen.

Bear's coffin was draped with beautiful flowers gathered from his property. Starfinder had drawn the Grateful Dead logo of a skull and a thirteen-point lightning bolt on the wooden coffin as if it were a piece of equipment Bear had marked for identification. A small laptop was next to it so we could Skype with our Grateful Dead family in San Rafael. I sat with Jerry and Melissa on the side of the room opposite the podium. We held hands and cried. A program illustrated with Bear's artwork was handed out. In the background, "Black Peter" from *Bear's Choice* and "Attics of My Life" from *American Beauty* played.

Starfinder read a poem by Robert Hunter, "An Anthem
for the Bear":

> Augustus Owsley Stanley the Third
> being less a name, than a designation,
> the bearer of the appellation became,
> of his own inspiration, The Bear.
> Thus he became and thus remained
> and every old timer worth salt has
> a tale or two to tell regarding same:
> of the time The Bear did this or that
> incredibly singular, utterly apposite
> action without apology or shame
> to his own particular undying fame.
> Unreachable, unteachable, aflame
> in the light of his own magnificence
> reflected in deeds dwarfing the achievements
> of the run-of-the-mill creative sort
> by a factor of ten or more,
> King of Many Things was he
> of mortal physiology
> the soul's chemistry,
> geography, geology,
> not to mention the
> applied physics of sound,
> regarding which, deaf in one ear,
> he pronounced stereo to be
> a distraction affording only
> one perfect seat in the house
> upon which to work its elusive illusion
> setting himself to design the world's
> most powerful hi-fi system to prove it!
> One suspects that, had he but one leg
> he'd have seen the advantage in that
> and invented accordingly, ingeniously
> and, it goes without saying, successfully.

Lovable and loving in the abstract
effusiveness was not his hole card;
his judgments swift, certain and irrevocable
the last word was his personal property.
For the few times he was wrong
there is no accounting.
Was there ever a man who changed so many
while, himself, changing so little?
A Cardinal Sign, were there ever one,
fixed like a bright white star in dark-blue heaven.
Save sentimental eulogies for lesser men
and leave it that he was King of Many Things
of perfected personal taste and detailed opinion
first and last a scientist and propounder
of a brand new species of reason.
No bucolic Heaven for such as Bear,
rather a Rock of Ages from where
an eagle in full flight might dare
a sudden detour into endless dawn.

Sail on, dear brother Bear, sail on.

If you wish your individuality to have meaning for others, then your identity must have continuity.*

I woke up the next morning in the tent I always stayed in and wandered up the crooked path of stone and dirt along the Walsh River to Bear's kitchen, hearing the curious hum of the eucalyptus trees, knowing that the best coffee could be percolating and an interesting stranger was probably asleep on the futon.

I did not want to leave Australia. At Bear's compound, his vibe was present. His older daughter from his first

*I Ching, Hexagram 32

marriage was rearranging her suitcases to optimize baggage for her return to the United States on the futon in front of the TV, and Starfinder was warming up the espresso machine while his wife breastfed the baby on the couch. Soon Melissa came and then Redbird and the boys. No one would let the widow, Sheilah, do any work. We were family bounded by grief, yes—but also framed by Owsley's inspiration and his teaching us a sense of comfort in change. The passion for change was ignited by the psychedelic revolution of the sixties, fueled by rock 'n' roll and LSD, and changed history.

We went our separate ways. I climbed up the short ladder to Bear's library, a sealed steel bubble with a heavy sliding-glass door and a lock. I was impressed with the quality of his books and their excellent condition despite life in the tropical Bush. He had old chemistry tomes with black-and-white diagrams, electrical engineering and metallurgy texts, manuscripts of books on the sixties and many hard copies of these, including *Bill Graham Presents* by Bill Graham and Robert Greenwood. He had books on plants and magic mushrooms; volumes on the mysteries of the Pyramids, the Obelisks, and the monuments of Mars; fantasy and science fiction paperbacks; heavy alchemical texts; and what looked like a PhD thesis, bound papers with an italicized, typed title on the binding, "At the Ends of the Earth." I turned my eyes and spied a more recognizable book, *Birds of Prey*, from our library in our house in Berkeley.

I flew first class back to New York. I carried with me the awareness of how my love for Owsley, this singular man, had directed my life. How different the details of my daily life were from Bear's in the Bush, yet how much the same. In focus, in attention to the details of full consciousness and faith in the generative power of psychedelics, in authentic living, in choosing any way of letting go as long as I did no harm, I was the same as Owsley. I lived in upstate New York, near Woodstock, a safe haven for the sixties generation and our children, a sacred place full of creative people and spiritual beings, artists, writers, musicians, dancers. My home is a round tower, hand-built by a sculptor who works in circus and believes in magic. And in my magic tower, I built an holistic practice of orthodontics with a fully equipped dental lab to fabricate orthodontic appliances. Helping Owsley build the most powerful sound system in the universe, I had learned to solder.

After the Dead at Golden Gate Park   © *Alvan Meyerowitz*

Afterword

My first memory of Tom Davis is at the Tanglewood Music Festival, summer 2006. We were there to celebrate Jon McIntire's sixty-fifth birthday. I had given Jon, a former manager of the Grateful Dead, a dozen tickets for his chosen friends to celebrate his birthday at the premier performance of an avant-garde composer. Tom Davis, Jon's friend, wouldn't accept a ticket. He would not commit to coming. If he could make it, he'd buy his own ticket. Tom Davis bounded up alone to the front gate at Tanglewood, full of energy, dancing rather than walking, tall and robust, long stylish hair and a beard. His voice was clear and sharp with a melodic timbre, fully embodied, and I heard him above the others.

Tom remembers our first meeting differently. He claims we met at the home of our publisher, Paul Cohen, and when a downpour suddenly burst from the sky, took refuge in a sheltered gazebo. For hours, with nothing to do, stuck in a small space, only three or four of us, we bonded. Tom's story is much more poetic, has a beginning, a middle, and an end, connects us to the future—a great sketch, even if it stretches the truth. So like Tom.

We attended exhibits of rock'n'roll posters; we went to shows. Anything to do with Grateful Dead music we shared. Our conversation never flagged. He was finishing his memoir, *Thirty-Nine Years of Short-Term Memory Loss*, and I was at my chronic task of writing *Owsley and Me*. I told him that when Jerry Garcia died in 1995, I sent zillions of emails to members of the Grateful Dead and to Grateful Dead family, declaring that the Grateful Dead must go on. Then I heard Garcia's voice saying, if you feel that strongly, write your own story. I told him how my efforts at collaboration had failed. I felt that Garcia had brought Tom and me together. Tom did not.

When I told Owsley I had become friends with Tom Davis, he said, "How dare you! He was the one who turned Garcia on to the Persian."

Awed by Tom's pedigree, I ignored Bear. Tom and I exchanged writing. He had purposely written his book showing little emotion, letting the reader find the feeling, but my story was a soapy tearjerker. Tom became my editor and changed that. When the chemo he was getting for his head and neck cancer failed, he decided to be my coauthor. His health waned, but his natural brilliance at writing soared. His sharp wordsmithing, his understanding of comedy concepts and the nature of reaction, his outstanding ability at sketch design and dialogue, his dedication to the jewel of memory transformed *Owsley and Me*.

Rhoney Stanley

www.ingramcontent.com/pod-product-compliance
Lightning Source LLC
Jackson TN
JSHW011947131224
75386JS00042B/1589

* 9 7 8 0 9 8 3 3 5 8 9 3 0 *